Copyright 2020 by Claude Waters -All rights reserved.

No part of this book may be reproduced or transmitted in any form or by any means, electronic or mechanical, including photocopying and recording, or by any information storage and retrieval system, without permission in writing from the publisher. This is a work of fiction. Names, places, characters and incidents are either the product of the author's imagination or are used fictitiously, and any resemblance to any actual persons, living or dead, organizations, events or locales is entirely coincidental. The unauthorized reproduction or distribution of this copyrighted work is ilegal.

Disclaimer Notice:

Please note the information contained within this document is for educational and entertainment purposes only. All effort has been executed to present accurate, up to date, reliable, complete information. No warranties of any kind are declared or implied. Readers acknowledge that the author is not engaged in the rendering of legal, financial, medical, or professional advice. The content within this book has been derived from various sources. Please consult a licensed professional before attempting any techniques outlined in this book.

By reading this document, the reader agrees that under no circumstances is the author responsible for any losses, direct or indirect, that are incurred as a result of the use of the information contained within this document, including, but not limited to, errors, omissions, or inaccuracies.

CONTENTS

Introduction 6
Chapter 1. What is Inflammation and its causes? 8
Chapter 2. The Science Behind the Anti-Inflammatory Diet 10
Chapter 3. What causes inflammation? Factors to consider 12
Chapter 4. Signs of Inflammation 15
Chapter 5. The Benefits of Following an Anti-Inflammatory Diet 16
Chapter 6. Foods that reduce inflammation naturally: 20
Chapter 7. Common Misconceptions about the Anti-inflammatory Diet 25
Chapter 8. What Kind of Disease Inflammation Can Cause? 26
Chapter 9. Foods Good for Anti-Inflammatory Diet 29
Chapter 10. Tips on Transitioning to an Anti-Inflammatory Lifestyle 30
Chapter 11: Breakfast 31
    No Cook Overnight Oats 31
    Avocado Cup with Egg 31
    Mediterranean toast 32
    Instant Banana Oatmeal 32
    Almond Butter-Banana Smoothie 32
    Brown Sugar Cinnamon Oatmeal 33
    Buckwheat Pancakes with Vanilla Almond Milk 33
    Tomato Bruschetta with Basil 34
    Sweet Corn Muffins 34
    Scrambled Eggs with Mushrooms and Spinach 35
    Chia and Oat Breakfast Bran 35
    Faux Breakfast Hash Brown Cups 36
    Maple Mocha Frappe 36
    Breakfast Oatmeal in Slow Cooker 37
    Apple Cinnamon Overnight Oats 37
    Spinach Mushroom Omelette 38
    Breakfast Grains and Fruits 39
    Eggs with Cheese 39
    Hearty Orange Peach Smoothie 40
    Cheddar & Kale Frittata 40
    Spinach and Tomato Egg Scramble 41
    French Toast with Cinnamon Vanilla 41
    Mango and Coconut Oatmeal 42
    Hot Honey Porridge 42
Chapter 12. Sides 43
    Cauliflower and Potato Mash 43
    Grilled Asparagus 43
    Garlic Steamed Squash 44
    Satisfying Corn Cob 44
    Devilled Eggs 45
    Borders Apart Mexican Cauliflower Rice 45
    Egg and Bean Medley 46

Cheddar and Apple Panini Sandwich 46
Roasted Carrots 47
Fancy Red and White Sprouts 47
Garlic and Chive "Mash" 48
Crashing Asparagus Risotto with Microstock 49
Turkey and Melted Cheese Sandwich 49
Garlic and Broccoli Mishmash 50
Crunchy Creamy Mashed Sweet Potatoes 50
Ultimate Roast Potatoes 51
Personal and Intimate Soy Milk 51
Extremely Crazy Egg Devils 52
Green pea purée 52
Herbed Green Beans 53
Easy Lemon Roasted Radishes 53
Green beans with nuts 54
Beets stewed with apples 54
Cabbage quiche 55
Baked tomatoes 55

Chapter 13. Poultry 56
Chicken and Veggies 56
Hidden Valley Chicken Drummies 56
Lemon-Parsley Chicken Breast 57
Chicken and Brussels sprouts 57
Chicken Divan 58
Spicy Pulled Chicken Wraps 58
Apricot Chicken Wings 59
Chicken and Broccoli 59
Balsamic roast chicken 60
Chicken, Bell Pepper & Spinach Frittata 60
Hot chicken wings 61
Balsamic Chicken and Beans 61
Butter Chicken 62
Five-Spice Roasted Duck Breasts 62
Chicken and Radish Mix 63
Chicken with Broccoli 63
Chicken, pasta and snow peas 64
Roast Chicken Dal 64
Stovetop Barbecued Chicken Bites 65
Peach Chicken Treat 65
Baked Chicken Pesto 66
Chicken and Avocado Bake 66
Chicken Chopstick 67
Champion Chicken Pockets 67

Chapter 14. Seafood 68
Lemony Mussels 68
Hot Tuna Steak 68

- Marinated Fish Steaks 69
- Baked Tomato Hake 69
- Cheesy Tuna Pasta 70
- Herb-Coated Baked Cod with Honey 70
- Tender salmon in mustard sauce 71
- Broiled White Sea Bass 71
- STEAMED FISH BALL 72
- Spicy baked fish 72
- LEMONY & CREAMY TILAPIA 72
- Smoked Trout Spread 73
- Broiled sea bass 73
- Spicy Cod 73
- Lemon Salmon with Kaffir Lime 74
- Heartfelt Tuna Melt 74
- Crab Salad 75
- Minty Cod Mix 75
- Salmon and Dill Capers 75
- Creamy Sea Bass Mix 76
- Tuna and Shallots 76
- Paprika Tuna 76
- Ginger Sea Bass Mix 77
- Parmesan Cod Mix 77

Chapter 15. Meat Recipes 78
- Lime Pork and Green Beans 78
- Pork with Lemongrass 78
- Pork with Olives 79
- Pork Chops with Tomato Salsa 79
- Mustard Pork Mix 80
- Pork with Chili Zucchinis and Tomatoes 80
- Pork with Thyme Sweet Potatoes 81
- Pork with Pears and Ginger 81
- Parsley Pork and Artichokes 82
- Pork with Mushrooms and Cucumbers 82
- Oregano Pork 83
- Creamy Pork and Tomatoes 83
- Pork with Balsamic Onion Sauce 84
- Ground Pork Pan 84
- Pork with Nutmeg Squash 85
- Pork with Cabbage and Kale 85
- Pork Salad 86
- Curry Pork Mix 86
- Italian Pork 87

Chapter 16. Smoothies and beverages 88
- Veggie Poached Eggs 88
- Baked Veggie Omelette 88
- Apple Omelette 89

Smoked Salmon Scramble 89
No-Bake Veggie Frittata 90
Choco Loco Tea Drink 90
Iced Matcha 91
Turmeric-Spiced Coconut Milk Shake 91
Pomegranate-Avocado Smoothie 91
Oats, Flaxseeds and Banana Smoothie 92
Berry Red Smoothie 92
Pineapple Banana-Oat Smoothie 93
Pineapple-Lettuce Smoothie 93
Spiced Carrot Smoothie 94
Mango, Cucumber and Spinach Smoothie 94
Grape-Avocado Smoothie 95
Spiced Pumpkin Smoothie 95
Almond and Pear Smoothie 96
Berry Nutty Smoothie 96

Chapter 17. Salads Recipes 97
Chickpeas Salad 97
Quinoa and Beans 97
Cucumber and Green Onions Salad 98
Barley and Kale 98
Herbed Mango Mix 99
Cabbage Slaw 99
Cucumber with Apples Salad 100
Parsley Avocado Mix 100
Endives and Broccoli 101
Arugula Salad 101
Mint Tomatoes and Onions Mix 102
Radish Salad 102
Green Beans and Okra 103
Tomato and Celery Mix 103
Corn and Avocado Mix 104
Chicken Salad with Cashew Cream 104
Chicken, Bok Choy & Jicama Salad 105
Chicken & Cabbage Salad 106
Chicken & Broccoli Salad 107
Beef & Broccoli Salad 108
Smoked Salmon & Veggie Salad 109
Salmon, Orange & Beet Salad 110
Salmon, Spinach & Kale Salad 111
Salmon & Tomato Salad 112
Salmon & Beans Salad 113

INTRODUCTION

Eating an anti-inflammatory diet is the top of the list to control inflammation. Anti-inflammatory diets on vegetables, whole grains, nuts, oily fish, some proteins, spices like ginger and turmeric, and brightly colored fruits will be heavy. Personally, I add an inflammation-fighting mangosteen product. Saturated fats, Tran's fats, maize and soybean oil, refined carbohydrates, sugars, red meat and dairy are the foods that promote inflammation. Now you see why with an anti-inflammatory diet you are likely to lose weight as well. An added advantage.

What's great with your diet to control inflammation is no side effects. No list of side effects with most drugs. And in just a few weeks you should see improvement.

A diet that is focused on anti-inflammatory principles is very helpful and is highly recommended. There is a study that having this diet not only can protect you in diseases but also slow the process of aging by maintaining your blood sugar and increasing metabolism.

Optimize your health with an anti-inflammatory diet. You should incorporate the anti-inflammatory principles:

Fiber-rich foods – Reduce inflammation by eating foods rich in fiber like fruits and vegetables. You can also get it from whole grains like oatmeal and barley.

8 servings of fruits and vegetables everyday – Increase your intake of garlic, onions, leek, broccoli, cabbage and cauliflower.

Stay away from saturated fats – Limit your red meat intake and use herbs and spices when you marinate meats to reduce the toxins formed when cooking.

Avoid processed foods and refined sugar – Artificial sweeteners and foods high in sodium are bad for your health and can trigger inflammation throughout the body. It can also cause other diseases like high blood pressure and increased insulin resistance.

Avoid trans fats – Saturated fats are no good but so are trans-fat. You need to avoid these kinds of fats because of the higher the trans-fat in the body, the higher the c-reactive protein that is a marker for inflammation in the body.

Omega -3 fatty acids – Consume foods that are rich in omegas-3 fatty acids like nuts, flax seeds, and beans. You can also take omega-3 supplements, but make sure that it is the best quality.

Use oils with health fats – Organic oils such as virgin and extra virgin olive oil are good choices. You can also use sunflower oil and canola. It has the best anti-inflammatory benefits.

Inflammation plays a part in so many diseases and has proven its association with the immune system. We may not understand how it really works, but it is really visible by what you eat. Poor diet adds to its causes. Be empowered and limit the amount of inflammation in your body.

This cookbook is not only for people who already have inflammation or auto-immune disorders but also for people who want to promote their overall well-being. Now that you are familiar with inflammation and what it can do to our body, get to know more about the Instant Pot. Instant Pot will be your partner in this endeavor to reduce inflammation.

It is a well-known fact that different foods are metabolized differently, some of which promote inflammation and some of which reduce it. The anti-inflammatory diet is aimed at promoting optimal health and healing by selecting foods that reduce inflammation. If one can control excessive inflammation by natural means (like by diet) successfully, it reduces one's dependence on anti-inflammatory drugs that have unwanted and unhealthy side effects and does not solve the underlying problem. Although anti-inflammatory drugs (such as NSAIDs) are a quick fix to alleviate symptoms, they ultimately weaken the immune system by damaging the gastrointestinal tract that plays an important role in the function of the immune system.

CHAPTER 1. WHAT IS INFLAMMATION AND ITS CAUSES?

Inflammation occurs when the body releases white blood cells to protect your body from unknown substances like foreign body contamination. It is specifically released to the injured or infected part of the body. Part of the body becomes red and swollen because the release of chemicals affects the blood flow.

There are good and bad aspects of inflammation. Yes, you read it right. Not all inflammation is bad. There are two types of inflammation and that is acute and chronic inflammation.

Acute inflammation occurs when you have a sprain or sore throat. In this kind of inflammation, you are assured that the body is repairing itself and the inflammation will go away when your body is repaired. It seems that inflammation is good to the body, however, there are times that the defense mechanism seems to crash. When it crashes, the inflammatory response is being set in motion even if there is no foreign body contamination. It is what happens when you have arthritis. Chronic inflammation is a different story. It takes several days and stays for a long time, leading to inflammatory diseases.

When the body has inflammation, it reacts to an injury, it sends cells to fight the invading foreign objects. The immune system is being damaged and harmed. Instead of protecting the body, it causes harm and problems in the body.

There are several factors that cause inflammation and one of the major causes of it is being linked to poor lifestyle choices.

Poor diet – Are you fond of eating sugary foods? Is eating in fast-food chains one of your favorites? Eating unhealthy foods can trigger inflammation together with fat and increased blood sugar. A poor diet can result with higher weight or weight gain. It is known that having a higher body fat can result in several diseases that we don't want to have. It is important to eat healthy so we can decrease our body fat. When we improve our diet, we make it better by decreasing the body's inflammatory response. This makes our body more efficient in managing potential complications of our weight gain.

Aging – It is still controversial how aging affects inflammation, but according to science, the progressive degenerative process is tightly integrated with inflammation. As our body age, there are several body cells that are starting to die. They cannot regenerate itself. So, when cells die, it becomes waste material or foreign substance in our body that can trigger inflammation.

Lack of physical activity – Lack of physical activity can result in obesity and overweight. There is really a link between your lifestyle and your weight. Your unhealthy lifestyle can cause changes to your physiological response to inflammatory factors. Obesity, for instance, results in low-grade chronic inflammation.

Poor sleep – Having a good night's sleep is a good way to start our day but what if we are sleep deprived over a long period of time? Sleep deprivation can cause physical changes in our brain and our body that can lead to arthritis, periodontitis, and cancer. It can contribute to chronic diseases and mental health issues. Study shows that having less than 7-8 hours of sleep increases inflammation. It is also been linked in having chronic diseases like heart problems, diabetes and hypertension.

Stress – Emotional, physical or psychological stress is not good for you! All of that can raise cortisol in your body. Cortisol is a hormone that is produced by the adrenal glands. The higher level of cortisol can create inflammation. Studies found that chronic stress affects the body by altering immune cells activity. When you reduce stress, you live healthier.

Smoking – We all know that smoking is not good for the body. Smoking affects and triggers an immunologic response to vascular injury that is known to be linked with increased levels of inflammatory markers. Inflammatory markers are white blood cells and c-reactive protein.

There are a lot of factors affecting our body and its link to having inflammation. Thus, it is necessary that we make to the things that we can control like turning to healthier options, changing our lifestyles and reducing our stress.

I believe that now that you have an idea of how chronic inflammation can harm your body, you are more interested in the recipes that can help you achieve a sustainable living.

CHAPTER 2. THE SCIENCE BEHIND THE ANTI-INFLAMMATORY DIET

When your body needs to respond to an injury, it tends to mobilize an army of specialized cells to fend of the invading organism and toxins.

These cells prepare pathways for fighter cells to attack and completely engulf the attackers.

Once that has happened, another group of cells tends to signal to the body and let it know the fighter cells have accomplished their task and the body is allowed to stop the production of preparatory and fighter cells.

These results a sort of cleanup that clears up the leftover fighter cells from the battlefield and repairs any damage.

Simply put, there are two steps to this response:

Pro-Inflammatory

Anti-Inflammatory

Each cell involved in the pro stage builds on the work of the previous cells and helps to make the immune reaction stronger for any upcoming attack.

During the pro period, symptoms such as redness, swelling, itching are common.

The anti-inflammatory is the reverse of pro-inflammatory and it works to lower the effects of inflammation.

A variety of substances used to block inflammation are made from essential fatty acids, which the body isn't able to produce on its own.

These acids must be obtained through supplements or foods.

Two essential ones are Omega-3 and Omega-6.

Omega-6 tends to increase inflammation while Omega-3 helps to reduce it.

It should be noted that what I wrote above is a simplified version of the whole mechanism and there is a lot more to it.

There are various substances that play a deeper role in the whole infrastructure that allows the body to control its inflammatory mechanism.

Some of the crucial ones are:

Histamine: White blood cells near an injury tend to release a substance known as histamine. They increase the permeability of blood vessels around the wound that signals fighter cells and other substances to regulate an immune response and come to the sight of injury. Histamine also causes redness and swelling around the affected region and causes runny nose, rash, itchy eyes.

Cytokines: These are proteins that are activated by pro-inflammatory eicosanoids to signal fighter cells to gather at the injury site. They are responsible for diverting energy from the body to catalyst the healing process. Release of these substances tend to cause tiredness and decrease appetite.

C-Reactive Protein: Cytokines alongside other pro-inflammatory eicosanoids are closely involved in the activation of a substance known as C-Reactive Protein. This particular organic compound produced by the liver responds to messages that are

sent out by white blood cells. The C-Reactive proteins tend to bind the site of injury and act as a sort of surveillance unit that helps to identify the invading bodies.
Leukocytes: Several types of leukocytes (also known as white blood cells) are critical to the process of neutralizing invading substances. Neutrophils, for example, are small, agile and are able to first arrive at the scene of the crime to ingest small microbes. However, large substances such as macrophages as required to tackle a large number of microbes.

There are a few more, but the gist still remains the same. When your body starts to suffer from an uncontrolled inflammation attack, the action of these and similar substances tend to get out of control, which results in extremely uncomfortable situations.

CHAPTER 3. WHAT CAUSES INFLAMMATION? FACTORS TO CONSIDER

The triggers of chronic inflammation can be very varied.
They are often related to each other, though.
It is important to know them because learning to detect them will make it easier for us to combat or avoid them.
These factors will be explained below:
Consuming unhealthy foods:
This is the factor that most often triggers chronic inflammation or at least, the one that most easily enhances its development.
The proper functioning of our body depends largely on our diet, which must be balanced and healthy.
The opposite only leads to our organism being altered.
We must not forget that we are what we eat.
If we eat well we will feel good and if we do it badly we will feel bad. That is a reality that we have to deal with day after day.
The right diet translates into more energy, more encouragement and a reduction in the likelihood of obesity, heart disease, diabetes and other health threats.
A diet lacking the nutrients necessary for our well-being and rich in fats and carbohydrates reduces our life expectancy and leads to obesity and other conditions, including chronic inflammation and all the underlying consequences of suffering it.
Intelligently the most convenient is to opt for the first option, right? For healthy eating?
Unfortunately junk food, refined flours and sugars, red meats, soft drinks and other harmful foods tempt us easily because of their pleasant taste.
It is easy to succumb to a bad diet but succumbing to unhealthy foods and eating too much of them will only lead to a host of diseases that we would really like to avoid. It will also lead to inflammation.
As we already know, chronic inflammation is very harmful. Its presence in our body can make us seriously ill.
Many foods frequently consumed by most people trigger a wrong inflammatory reaction.
Our organism simply does not know these "foods" as nutrients and sees them as a threat. It rejects them.
The reality is that these foods are a poison to our body and enhance inflammation.
Here is a list of foods to avoid, to prevent and fight inflammation:
Foods that cause inflammation:
Refined flours
Refined sugar
Red meat
Sausages

Hydrogen oils
Refreshments
Dairy products (Butter, margarine, too fatty cheeses)
Junk food
Alcohol
And in general, processed foods
Reducing the consumption of these foods is vital in the fight against inflammation and its prevention.
Overweight:
Obesity and inflammation are related.
Chronic inflammation produces obesity and vice versa.
What is certain is that overweight generates inflammatory reactions in the intestine, abdomen and in the organism in general.
If we do not do something about it, the inflammatory reaction triggered by obesity will remain in our body longer than it should and there will appear the feared chronic inflammation.
This factor is closely related to the one explained above.
A diet based on flour, refined sugar and other foods harmful to health, such as those with excess fat or carbohydrates will lead us to obesity and consequently will cause us to suffer chronic inflammation.
This establishes the importance of a healthy diet to avoid inflammation and its ills.
Sedentary life:
This factor that triggers chronic inflammation is related to the previous ones.
Poor nutrition and a sedentary lifestyle will lead to the development of obesity and, as an underlying consequence, chronic inflammation will be present.
When you lead a sedentary lifestyle, your body doesn't work the right way because we don't help you oxygenate as you should. As a result, the immune system is likely to weaken and not function as well.
The weakened immune system will have to work harder to try to combat the harmful agents and external agents that can make our bodies sick.
This can undoubtedly lead to chronic inflammation.
Smoking:
For no one it is a secret that smoking is harmful to health and one of the leading causes of death around the world.
This bad habit damages to a great extent our lungs and promotes cancer in them and the appearance of inflammatory diseases such as gingivitis, rhinitis and the like. It also damages our dental health by contributing to weakened teeth.
Not to mention the bad breath that smokers have to deal with.
Some think that the negative effects of smoking are only those stated above. But they are wrong.

Smoking also enhances chronic inflammation.
When we smoke, we let our lungs be bombarded by cigarette or tobacco smoke. Our brain detects the presence of that smoke as an invasion and in response to it our immune system activates the inflammatory process.
If we smoke too often, we will cause the body to trigger the process with the same frequency and sooner or later that causes the acute inflammation to become chronic.
Pollution:
Another of the triggers of chronic inflammation is pollution.
Another of the triggers of chronic inflammation is pollution.
With pollution something similar happens to what happens with the action of smoking.
Exposure to pollutants often causes our immune system to activate to protect us from everything it considers invasive: smoke, bacteria that can adhere to us and are found in the trash, viruses that circulate in polluted air, among others.
Over time, that body's natural reaction will become chronic because it has been activated for too long or in a very repetitive manner.

CHAPTER 4. SIGNS OF INFLAMMATION.

The main signs of inflammation include; heat, redness, pain, swelling, and muscle-function loss. These signs depend on the inflamed body part and its cause. Some of the widespread symptoms of chronic inflammation are:
- Frequent infections.
- Weight gain.
- Body pain.
- Insomnia
- Fatigue
- Mood disorders like anxiety and depression.
- Gastrointestinal problems like diarrhea, constipation, and acid reflux disease.

The typical signs of inflammation rely on various inflammatory effect problems. When the body defends mechanism which influences the skin, it causes rashes. When you are dealing with arthritis rheumatoid, it affects the joints. Most of the signs and symptoms experienced are made up of fatigue, tingling, joint pains, stiffness, and swelling.

Similarly, when experiencing inflammatory bowel, it typically influences the digestive system. Its usual signs consist of bleeding ulcers, anemia, weight loss, bloating, pains, diarrhea, and stomach pains. With multiple sclerosis, the condition occurs on the myelin sheath, which covers the nerve cells. Its signs consist of problems when passing out stool, double vision, blurred eyesight, fatigue, and cognitive issues.

If you are facing any of the signs above and the health problems, you could be suffering from inflammation. Many people link it to joint pains like those of arthritis, which can be signaled by swelling and aches. The problem is related to health problems, not just swollen joints. Nevertheless, all soreness is not bad. For instance, acute inflammation is vital throughout recovery from a twisted and puffy ankle.

It is easy to detect Chronic inflammation signs and causes. Insomnia, genetic predisposition, your food intake, and other individual habits can cause it. Similarly, inflammation resulting from allergic may also develop in your gut.

Below are some of the possibilities that you may be having it;
- If you always feel fatigued to the extent of not having enough sleep, not getting enough nap, or you sleep excessively.
- Do you experience time-to-time aches and pains? This may also signify that you have arthritis.
- Are you experiencing any pain in the gut or stomachache? The pain may create inflammation. Gut inflammation may also cause cramping, bloating, and loose stools.
- A puffy lymph node is another sign of inflammation. These nodes lie in the neck, armpits, and groin, which swell in case there is a problem in your system. When you have a sore throat, your neck nodes lump because the body's defense system has sensed the condition. These lymph nodes react since the body is fighting the infection. The nodes reshape as you heal.
- Is your nose stuffed up? If indeed, maybe it is a symptom of irritating nasal tooth cavities.
- Sometimes, your epidermis may protrude because of internal inflammation.

CHAPTER 5. THE BENEFITS OF FOLLOWING AN ANTI-INFLAMMATORY DIET

Health and Lifestyle Benefits of Anti-Inflammatory Foods

Once you begin to implement foods with a high nutrient level and anti-inflammatory properties, you'll notice significant benefits often within one or two weeks. If you normally experience bloating and/or inflammation, you'll notice these symptoms will reduce and may disappear altogether. Over a longer time, you may notice the benefits of weight loss, improved energy, and a reduction in symptoms from a variety of health conditions. Following an anti-inflammatory diet should not be considered a temporary fix or a quick solution, but rather a long-term commitment that fits into your lifestyle.

How do Anti-Inflammatory Foods Work?

People who tend to follow a Mediterranean diet or consume plant-based foods only will naturally alleviate stress on the body and, therefore, prevent occurrences of inflammation. This also prevents the onset of diseases and conditions that develop as we age, and help improve how we function and focus as we grow older. Regular exercise, drinking plenty of water, and avoiding processed and sugary foods are also excellent ways to prevent disease and improve overall health. Inflammation occurs as a response to our body's immune system, as a trigger when something isn't right. When we become inflamed, it's our body's way of trying to fight an infection or condition as a natural immune response. When this happens frequently and over a longer period of time, this process becomes a trigger for other diseases and conditions, such as Alzheimer's, depression, and diabetes. It can also lead to stroke and heart disease if left untreated. Many people take medication for the treatment of inflammation, though in the long-term, it only resolves the symptoms temporarily, while further damage is done within the body. For this reason, taking a more preventative approach to your health and bodily functions is key to living the best quality of life as possible.

Focus on Healthy Nuts and Seeds

Whether your focus is eating leaner meats, including fish and poultry, or consuming a plant-based diet, all can agree that nuts and seeds should become a mainstay in your way of eating, due to the sheer number of nutrients and minerals they contain, and in such small amounts. Just a small portion of nuts and/or seeds each day can replace some vitamin supplements while providing a nutritious snack. Making these small, but mighty foods a center of your diet is a good way to make the anti-inflammatory way of eating a successful lifestyle. To become more familiar with the benefits of nuts and seeds, research as much as possible, so that you know exactly which varieties to include, not just based on nutrients, but on taste and preference. Almonds pack a good dose of protein, vitamin E, magnesium, and fiber. They contain very little carbohydrates and can improve cholesterol levels. In addition to having anti-inflammatory properties, almonds assist in weight loss and improving metabolism. They reduce blood pressure and improve blood sugar levels. This variety of nuts is ideal for people who have type 2 diabetes.

Walnuts are popular and used in a lot of desserts and as a salad topping. They contain a significant amount of healthy fats and fiber, making them ideal for weight loss and maintenance. Like almonds, they regulate blood sugar and improve metabolism, while preventing heart disease and other chronic conditions.

Pistachios are distinguishable by their greenish color once they are removed from their shells, and are often added to desserts, puddings, and drinks, including smoothies. They make a great topping to many dishes and can also be enjoyed as a snack, roasted or raw. Pistachios help improve heart health and provide a significant amount of healthy fats for overall bodily function. Blood pressure and glucose levels are lowered, and weight loss is also improved.

Pecans are one of the favorite nuts added to desserts, because of their pleasant texture and taste combination. They are often seen in butter tarts or pies, including ice creams and other treats. Pecans make a great snack on-the-go and provide a healthy dose of magnesium, which is essential for bone and muscle health. They are high in antioxidants and contain polyphenols, which are essentially antioxidants, which improve the quality of blood in the body while improving cholesterol levels.

Macadamia nuts are one of the tops options for heart health, as they contain a high amount of monounsaturated fats and keep cholesterol levels normal. While they are an expensive option compared to other nut varieties, macadamia nuts can be found in bulk stores and enjoyed in small portions, as well as in recipes.

Cashews are tasty raw or toasted, and often one of the most enjoyed snacks on their own. They are filling and make a great snack on their own, or mixed with other nuts and seeds. Metabolism and antioxidant performance have been noted in studies resulting from the consumption of cashews, as well as other nuts with similar nutrients. Cashews are high in fats and help regulate blood sugar and cholesterol.

Brazil nuts originate from the Amazon and contain selenium, a mineral that is also an antioxidant. Deficiency in selenium can lead to a number of diseases and conditions, which makes it vital for overall health and bodily function. It helps regulate your body's weight and metabolism.

Hazelnuts are one of the top options for spreads and additions to chocolate desserts and can be helpful in reducing the chances of heart disease. Hazelnuts are high in vitamin E and improve the blood vessel function in the body.

Peanuts are one of the most popular and common nuts used in recipes and everyday snacks. They are often found prepacked with salt and/or other flavors. For maximum benefits, peanuts are best consumed raw or lightly roasted, without any added salt or sugars. While they can trigger an allergic reaction for some people, they are generally safe for anyone who doesn't have any conditions impacted by peanuts. They are a good option for women who are pregnant, as regular consumption may reduce the likelihood of peanut allergies in children. This may also reduce the prevalence of childhood asthma as well. Peanut butter is another excellent option, provided no additional sugar, salt, or preservatives are added.

Seeds, like nuts, provide many health benefits and should be consumed as regularly as possible. Not all seeds may seem likely to become a part of your diet, though rotating them and trying a few varieties can give you a good idea of which ones you'd like to use more often. Some seeds are great as snacks on their own, such as sunflower or pumpkin seeds, while chia seeds, flax, and hemp seeds are used as ingredients in cereals, smoothies, and salads.

Chia seeds are small, tiny, black or reddish-brown seeds that have become more popular in recent years due to their high levels of nutrients. Just one small serving of chia seeds contains antioxidants, protein, calcium, magnesium, omega 3 and 6s, vitamin B1, and manganese. The increased production of ALA in the blood directly reduces the prevalence of inflammation, which is the effect of chia seeds in the body. Reducing blood sugar, improving type 2 diabetes symptoms, and reducing the likelihood of heart disease are among many other benefits of chia seeds. Fortunately, you don't have to eat large amounts to reap the benefits, though a regular, small portion of your daily routine will go a long way to improving your health overall.

Hemp seeds are an excellent source of protein and fatty acids. They contain important nutrients your body can't produce, which makes hemp an advantage to include in your diet. The quality of protein in hemp is considered high, which makes it a good option as a boost to smoothies. Some bulk stores and natural foods stores offer hemp protein powder as a supplement for vegan bodybuilding and as a powder to add to drinks, milkshakes, and smoothies. Hemp also helps improve skin health and can fight against eczema, as well as improving the moisture levels in the skin. Some people have shown a significant decrease in eczema symptoms after regular hemp use.

Flaxseeds are best to consume ground, rather than as whole seeds, in order to get the most out of their nutritious ingredients. High in antioxidants, fiber, and healthy fats, flaxseeds are often added to cereals, both hot and cold, to boost the nutrition value. They can also be added to smoothies like hemp and chia seeds. There are some studies that indicate possible prevention and treatment of tumors in some cases, which is promising for people who suffer from both benign and cancerous tumor growth.

Sesame seeds are often enjoyed as a topping on desserts, bagels, bread, or stir fry dishes. They are most popular lightly toasted and can blend in with many different dishes and flavors. Some studies indicate possible prevention of heart disease and cancer due to the high level of antioxidants. They also reduce inflammation, which provides relief from the effects of arthritis, including pain management. Consuming just a small portion of sesame seeds and/or powder each week can significantly reduce the inflammatory properties in the body. This can help improve and heal muscle stress and damage in athletes, which makes sesame powders and butter another great way to get a good dose of protein and healing properties for your body.

Pumpkin seeds are an excellent snack on-the-go, either raw or lightly roasted, without salt. They contain phytosterols, which contribute to lower blood sugar and the likelihood of breast cancer. Pumpkin seeds have shown positive results in the treatment and prevention of both bladder and kidney stones. Prevention occurs due to the seeds' ability to lower the amount of calcium in the urine, which contributes to the formation of stones. This also has the effect of improving prostate and urinary tract function, preventing disease and infection. Women may experience relief from menopause symptoms and lowering cholesterol.

Sunflower seeds are a tasty seed full of vitamins and healthy fats. There seems to be a significant amount of inflammation reduction, specifically in older adults, as well as reducing heart disease and other conditions associated with inflammation. While sunflower seeds are beneficial to anyone, they are especially helpful for aging adults over the age of 50, who are prone to more chronic conditions and health issues. Other studies show promising results in post-menopausal women who have type 2 diabetes, as well as lowering and regulating cholesterol levels.

In general, unless you experience adverse reactions or severe allergies to nuts or seeds, add as many varieties as possible into your diet as a regular staple. In fact, use nuts and seeds as the centerpiece of your diet and build your fruits, vegetables, and meat or vegan proteins around them. Making nuts and seeds the focus of your diet has many benefits in itself, for more reasons than health:

Nuts and seeds are portable and can be easily added to any dishes at home or on the go.

While some nuts and seeds are expensive, many can be purchased in bulk, making them easier to control in terms of portion and consumption. This will help you plan your budget around the foods you eat, to include portions and costs.

They are easy as a snack and when you are in a crunch for a meal. If you don't have time for breakfast in the morning or might skip a meal at the point in the day, a handful of nuts and/or seeds can fill the gap until you have the chance to enjoy a full meal.

Yogurt, oatmeal, salads, and smoothies are just some of the foods you can add nuts and seeds too, even when you don't have time to make them at home. For example, a take-out salad from the local restaurant or café near work can easily be topped with a few teaspoons of chia seeds, pistachios, and/or peanuts.

CHAPTER 6. FOODS THAT REDUCE INFLAMMATION NATURALLY:

When it comes to eating with an eye towards anti-inflammatory foods, there are plenty of options when it comes to avoiding the multitude of harmful products that contain inflammatory producing agents that can broadly be broken down into a handful of categories. Commit the following guidelines for the foods to eat and the foods to avoid to memory and you will be inflammation free in no time flat.

Eat more fiber: Studies show that a diet which is high in fiber is naturally going to create an overall lower level of inflammation because of all of the phytonutrients that natural unprocessed foods including fruits and vegetables have in spades. To ensure you consume 25 grams of fiber per day, make a point of eating lots of blueberries 3.5 grams bananas 3 grams onions, eggplant, okra, oatmeal, and barley.

Aim for 9 servings of vegetables and fruits every day: Make a point of consuming a ratio of 2 to 1 vegetable when compared to fruits as too many fruits in a single day can cause your total sugar intake to increase rapidly. A serving is generally considered half a c of cooked vegetables or 1 c of raw vegetables. Both ginger and turmeric are known to fight inflammation as well and both make great seasonings.

Aim for 4 servings of crucifers and alliums each week: Alliums are things like leeks, onions, scallions, and garlic while crucifers comprise numerous vegetables including Brussels sprouts, mustard greens, cauliflower, cabbage, and broccoli. These all contain extremely high levels of antioxidants, which is why only a few each week is enough to significantly lower your risk of inflammation-related cancer when consumed regularly. Remember, 4 servings a week is the minimum when it comes to alliums and crucifers, the more the merrier.

Keep saturated fat to a minimum: In order to start actively reducing the amount of inflammation in your body, it is important that you start keeping a close eye on the number of saturated fats that you are consuming on a daily basis. This means cutting it to 10 percent of the total number of calories that you consume in a day. This means you will likely want to cut down on the red meat and stick with health marinates made from anti-inflammatory spices instead of Coconut oil.

Eat lots of omega-3 fatty acids: As previously discussed, eating more omega-3 fatty acids should be at the top of the list of anyone who is interested in decreasing their inflammation level. In addition to being found in fish, it is also found in large doses in walnuts, flaxseeds and soy, kidney and navy beans. A regular omega-3 supplement is also recommended. When it comes to fish, anchovies, sardines, trout, mackerel, herring, oysters and salmon all contain the highest amounts of omega-3 and you should aim to eat 3 of them each week. Seek out healthy fats: Fats have gotten somewhat of a bad rap over the years because at some point mainstream society decided to start lumping all fats together. In truth, there are healthy fats which are a good source of energy for those who eschew carbohydrates in favor of a more natural energy solution. This means that plenty of healthy fats like those found in coconut oil, coconut oil and pressed canola oil are a great way to eat healthy while still expelling inflammatory elements from your system. Avoid product made with corn syrup and/or refined sugar: Studies show that simply adding a daily dose of processed foods to your diet by eating things that are dosed with high amounts of sugar or corn syrup is enough to increase your inflammation levels significantly.

Unfortunately, processed food companies understand that the more sugar something has in it the more likely it is to sell which means that it is virtually impossible to find anything processed that has enough sugar or corn syrup in it to cause inflammation in at least 2 full-grown adults. This intense fructose overload is enough to cause inflammation in the lining of blood vessels and should be avoided whenever possible.

Avoid trans-fat: In addition to saturated fats, it is important to avoid trans-fats as often as possible. This means looking at product labels as trans-fats are often hiding under the label of partially hydrogenated oils. Trans-fats are known to cause inflammation in the cell lining of the arteries as well as lower beneficial cholesterol levels which increase that of the harmful variety.

Avoid the wrong types of oil: In general, the healthy fat-based oils that are listed above are a healthy option, all others should be avoided regardless of the health claims they may tout. These oils are often extracted using chemicals that are known to increase inflammation and are rarely disclosed on product labels as they are used in the creation of the product and not added in after the fact. What's more, they are also typically high in omega-6 fatty acids, decreasing the balance in the body between that and omega-3 fatty acids and increasing inflammation in the process.

Avoid refined carbohydrates: While complex carbohydrates are a great source of energy, refined carbohydrates are typically simple carbohydrates which means they break down extremely quickly while also being responsible for the low energy feeling related to a sugar crash. What's more, the refining process is simply another word for the processing which means they are stripped of what little nutritional value that they would otherwise have. They are also typically high in sugar which makes them a trigger for inflammation in just about every possible way imaginable.

Avoid too much alcohol: When consumed to excess, both beer and hard alcohol have been linked to an increase in inflammation if used regularly. A good rule of thumb is that men should stick with no more than 2 drinks per day and women should limit themselves to 1 drink if they want to drink while at the same time keep their inflammation levels to a minimum.

Overuse of anti-inflammatory drugs can cause harmful side effects to the body. Therefore, the best option to fight inflammation is to do so through food.

A wide variety of foods have anti-inflammatory or antioxidant properties that can help us get rid of inflammation or prevent it naturally.

These foods are effective both in reducing the annoying symptoms present in acute inflammation and in minimizing the likelihood of suffering chronic inflammation or, when reducing the sequelae that the latter can cause in the body.

These valuable foods and their specific health benefits are explained below:
-List of anti-inflammatory foods
1 - Foods rich in Omega 3:

Fatty fish:
Wild salmon
Trout
Sardines
Anchovies
Mackerel
2.- Seeds:
Linseed
Chia seeds:
Sesame seed:
Hemp:
Sunflower seeds
Fruits:
Pineapple
Lemon
Strawberries
Blueberries
Grapes
Papaya
Guava
Avocado
Kiwis
Dried fruits:
Nuts
Hazelnuts
Vegetables
Broccoli
Tomatoes
Cauliflower
Carrot
Garlic
Onions
Lettuce
Chard
Spinach
Radishes
Legumes
Soja
Peas
Chickpeas
Green beans
Black beans
Natural oils
Olive oil
Linseed oil
Avocado oil
Coconut oil
Spices:
Turmeric
Ginger
Cinnamon
Whole- grain cereal
Oats
Quinoa
Fermented Foods
Kombucha
Kefir
Miso
Mushrooms
Infusions
Green tea
Matcha tea
Lean Meats
List of anti-inflammatory foods and their health benefits
1 - Foods rich in Omega 3:
Fatty fish:
Wild salmon
Trout
Sardines
Anchovies
Mackerel
Herring

The whole variety of foods mentioned above are an important source of omega-3 fatty acids or healthy acids.

Omega-3, in medical science, has been shown to be effective in fighting arthritis symptoms, reducing asthma symptoms, and preventing heart disease.

Their important contributions to the improvement of the above-mentioned diseases are due to the fact that these acids are effective in reducing high cholesterol levels and that they have anti-inflammatory effects.

This nutrient is considered important for preventing or fighting chronic inflammation.

In addition to the above, these foods provide a significant amount of protein to the body. They are the perfect substitute for red meats whose excessive consumption can have serious consequences for health.

They are ideal to include in any meal. Either breakfast, lunch or dinner and can be accompanied by many other healthy foods such as all the existing variety of vegetables or mushrooms.

It is best to eat them roasted or baked.

Linseed

These are seeds that have great popularity within dietary regimes and in cooking in general. They are seeds with important medicinal properties.

Flaxseed or flaxseed are seeds of high nutritional value that we can take advantage of very much.

Within the anti-inflammatory diets and even within the diets to lose weight their presence cannot be missing.

Among the set of edible seeds, they are among the healthiest and most favorable.

They contain high levels of fiber, healthy fatty acids such as omega 3, which is present in at least 55 percent of its nutritional content, vitamins such as vitamin E and various minerals such as phosphorus, iron, potassium and others.

They also contain important contributions of vegetable protein.

Inside our organism they exert a laxative effect that keeps our stomach clean and antioxidant and anti-inflammatory effects in general. They are also credited with promoting digestion by being able to reduce intestinal transit time.

At the same time, they are highly dietetic and suitable to be included in any diet thought to lose weight.

Adding a handful of these seeds to drinks and salads is enough to take advantage of their incredible benefits.

One of the most common ways to consume them is to add them to a glass of water and drink.

In that simple way we prepare a refreshing and very nutritious drink with a satiating effect that will help us avoid harmful temptations and combat the feared chronic inflammation.

- Chia seeds:

Adding a handful of these seeds to salads, smoothies and other recipes will greatly promote our health.

Chia seeds are considered a superfood, which means they have a lot of nutrients to give us. Their high concentration in mucilage (A type of healthy fiber) makes them ideal for promoting the proper functioning of the immune system because they help purify the body.

These substances lubricate the gastrointestinal tract, facilitating intestinal transit.

Therefore, they fight constipation and cleanse us of toxins.

A small handful of them has about 12 grams of this type of fiber so beneficial within anti-inflammatory diets.

In addition to fiber has antioxidants and various minerals such as calcium or boron. They also contain omega 3.

Their consumption allows us to comply with at least 3 of the principles of anti-inflammatory diets: Increased consumption of omega 3, increased consumption of soluble fibers and consumption of anti-inflammatory foods.

There is no doubt that these seeds are potent anti-inflammatory foods capable of curbing the ravages of chronic inflammation and reducing the symptoms of acute inflammation, which are really annoying.

There are no excuses not to include them in your diet. Just sprinkle them on your salads and drinks and your health will thank you very much.

Hemp:

Hemp seeds are considered a macronutrient because of their high content of vitamins, minerals and other components.

They are rich in magnesium, iron, essential fatty acids, protein, vitamin E and fiber.

Thanks to the fiber have laxative effects that improve the digestive system and the secretion of impurities, helping the body to cleanse.

Thanks to their vitamin E content, they fight free radicals, oxidation and inflammation.

Thanks to its content in fatty acids also improve the symptoms of many inflammatory diseases due to their inhibitory kindness of the inflammation process.

Sunflower seeds:

These seeds are found in the center of the flower called sunflower.

They are suitable for consumption and very rich in nutrients.

As they contain high values of vitamin E they are effective against inflammation and are attributed to improvements in the symptoms of inflammatory diseases such as asthma and rheumatoid arthritis.

You can eat them with yogurt along with nuts and other seeds, include them in salads or salad dressings and even in smoothies.

CHAPTER 7. COMMON MISCONCEPTIONS ABOUT THE ANTI-INFLAMMATORY DIET

There is no exact definition of an anti-inflammatory diet, and the definition depends on whom you ask. Consequently, there are a lot of misconceptions about this diet. Let`s clarify some myths for you to get rid of, and instead focus on what really matters to boost your health. Some of the major misunderstanding and mistakes about the anti-inflammatory diet are as follows:

An anti-inflammatory diet is a restrictive diet.

People trying to control their eating for one reason or another often end up with very strict diets. They create a list of foods to avoid and end up with joyless diets that may also compromise their nutritional intake. Sometimes, the very restrictive diets may even cause more health problems than they help. The truth of the matter is that anti-inflammatory diets are made up of a wide variety of foods and only work on limiting the amount of intake as opposed to the elimination of foods from your diets. This ensures you enjoy tasty meals in the right quantities without having to think too much about restricting foods.

Spicy foods cause inflammation.

This misconception comes from the middle ages. Many people believe that spicy foods are the cause of many health problems. The truth is some spices may worsen certain medical conditions, but there is not any scientific proof that spices cause diseases. So as you plan your anti-inflammatory diets ensure that you consider each food substance to be included as opposed to following such generalizations.

There is a one-fits-all recipe when it comes to anti-inflammatory diets

This is another misconception about the ability of many people to use anti-inflammatory diets. The truth is different people suffer from different kinds of inflammation caused by different agents. So, what works for one person may not work in a similar manner for another person. There are many conditions involved when it comes to inflammation, and this can affect how your body reacts to certain foods. It is very important to take this fact into account and experiment with various foods until you find what works for you. If you try a certain diet and find out that it does not work for you, don't just give up on the whole issue but try out other different meals to see if they work for you.

Milk causes inflammation.

There are a lot of reports that suggest that milk is bad for our health. Among the major claims in these reports is that milk causes inflammation. However, studies have shown that milk and other dairy products have anti-inflammatory properties and can actually protect from chronic inflammation. Therefore, it is important to consider including milk in your anti-inflammatory diets as it has been revealed to have immense benefits to your health.

Chapter 8. What Kind of Disease Inflammation Can Cause?

If we make a comparison, we would soon see that most of the causes of Inflammation are related to diet, so we are keeping this at the top of the list. Harmful substances such as refined fats, animal products, and refined carbohydrates cause damage in the long run. It should be noted though that carbohydrates do not directly contribute to inflammation, refined foods with higher concentration and fats are found to be naturally dense with inflammation-causing substances that affect the gut and increases inflammation.

The types of fat consumed by an individual also play a role here. Back in the early days, when everything was simple, people used to stay on a diet that was well-balanced on both Omega-3 and Omega-6 fats. However, modern diets tend to have a high concentration of Omega-6 fat as opposed to Omega-3 fat; this increases the possibility of suffering from inflammation by 10-20%. It is important for the body to have a good supply of Omega-3 fatty acids because the Omega-6 and Omega-3, both compete for the same COX enzymes, which are needed to build large fatty molecules.

COX-2 enzyme, in particular, is essential for making inflammatory prostaglandins. Too much Omega-6 fatty acids will result in the domination of this enzyme, and the body will not be able to utilize the enzyme anymore in conjunction with Omega-3 fats to reduce inflammation. Nowadays, fats are chemically modified, and this plays a greater role in inflammation as well.

They are made to be more inexpensive, which results in the production of highly inflammatory products. Aging The natural process of aging contributes to inflammation, as well. As we age, the body's cells can regenerate, but most of them start to die, leaving behind waste material that can trigger inflammation.

Obesity and Inactivity Excessive inactivity can and will often lead to obesity, which is a major cause of inflammation. Adipose tissue, the layer of fat that is found right under our skin, is actually responsible for much more than just keeping it warm. It is a metabolically active layer that causes the body to change the body chemistry and is also affected by the body's other systems.

The fat layer contains a large number of white blood cells and a greater level of fat. The cell count is linked together. Meaning, the more fat there is, the greater the number of white cells will be present. These cells often release pro-inflammatory substances that gradually contribute to the rise of inflammatory effects. Sleep Deprivation Researchers have shown that a lack of sleep is linked to the formation of certain infection-fighting white blood cells such as T-Cells.

Depriving ourselves of sleep will cause the number of T-Cells to decrease, which in turn increases the number of inflammation-promoting cytokines. Stress Cortisol is a hormone produced by adrenal glands and is used to manage the body's response to stress. It helps stimulate bursts of energy and suppresses pro-inflammatory substances.

This also helps to reduce stress by counteracting the effects of pro-inflammatory eicosanoids. However, if you stress too much, the amount of cortisol might increase to a dramatic level that will cause your immune cells to lose sensitivity to this hormone and trigger inflammation. Sun Exposure This might seem a little bit surprising, but excessive exposure to sunlight can often result in an individual suffering from inflammation. Sunburn or over-exposure encourages the formation of free radicals under the skin surface. Just to let you know, free radicals are unstable molecules that tend to destroy injury-fighting cells and lower the number of white blood cells present in the body. As you may have guessed, this lowers the strength of the body's immune system and leads to inflammatory attacks. Smoking Exposure to various toxins such as cigarette smoke plays a high role in inflammation. Either second hand or first hand, inhaled tobacco tends to cripple the body's capacity to fight diseases by suppressing the production of white blood cells. Craze Behind

Inflammation So, why are people heading for an anti-inflammatory diet? Despite having the best technology and health care services in the world, America is still suffering from an epidemic of chronic inflammation and other chronic inflammatory diseases.

The change in the form of a modern diet is contributing to increasing the number of incidents as well. When we are referring to chronic inflammation, we are implying various diseases such as arthritis, asthma among the long-term illnesses/diseases. Science of Inflammation Now that you have a little idea of just how severe of a problem inflammation is, let us have a look at how inflammation works, and what happens to your body during inflammation. When your body needs to respond to an injury, it tends to mobilize an army of specialized cells to fend of the invading organism and toxins. These cells prepare pathways for fighter cells to attack and completely engulf the attackers.

Once that has happened, another group of cells tends to signal to the body and let it know the fighter cells have accomplished their task, and the body is allowed to stop the production of preparatory and fighter cells. These result in a sort of cleanup that clears up the leftover fighter cells from the battlefield and repairs any damage. Simply put, there are two steps to this response: pro-inflammatory and anti-inflammatory. Each cell involved in the pro stage builds on the work of the previous cells and helps to make the immune reaction stronger for any upcoming attack. During the pro period, symptoms such as redness, swelling, itching are common. The anti-inflammatory is the reverse of pro-inflammatory, and it works to lower the effects of inflammation.

A variety of substances used to block inflammation are made from essential fatty acids, which the body isn't able to produce on its own. These acids must be obtained through supplements or foods.

Two essential ones are Omega-3 and Omega-6. Omega-6 tends to increase inflammation, while Omega-3 helps to reduce it. It should be noted that what I wrote above is a simplified version of the whole mechanism, and there is a lot more to it. There are various substances that play a deeper role in the whole infrastructure that allows the body to control its inflammatory mechanism. Some of the crucial ones are Histamine: White blood cells near an injury tend to release a substance known as histamine. They increase the permeability of blood vessels around the wound that signals fighter cells and other substances to regulate immune response and come to the sight of injury.

Histamine also causes redness and swelling around the affected region and causes runny nose, rash, itchy eyes. Cytokines: These are proteins that are activated by pro-inflammatory eicosanoids to signal fighter cells to gather at the injury site. They are responsible for diverting energy from the body to catalyst the healing process. The release of these substances tends to cause tiredness and decrease appetite. C-Reactive Protein: Cytokines alongside other pro-inflammatory eicosanoids are closely involved in the activation of a substance known as C-Reactive Protein.

This particular organic compound produced by the liver responds to messages that are sent out by white blood cells. The C-Reactive proteins tend to bind the site of injury and act as a sort of surveillance unit that helps to identify the invading bodies. Leukocytes: Several types of leukocytes (also known as white blood cells) are critical to the process of neutralizing invading substances. Neutrophils, for example, are small, agile and are able to first arrive at the scene of the crime to ingest small microbes.

However, large substances such as macrophages as required to tackle a large number of microbes. There are a few more, but the gist still remains the same. When your body starts to suffer from an uncontrolled inflammation attack, the action of these and similar substances tend to get out of control, which results in extremely uncomfortable situations. Harmful side effects of Inflammation Uncontrolled inflammation results in diseases that are known as autoimmune diseases. While there are a large number of them out there, some of the more prominent ones are Type 1 Diabetes: Type 1 Diabetes can cause the immune system to attack and destroy insulin-producing cells in your pancreas that disrupt the regulation of sugar levels in your body. Rheumatoid Arthritis: RA causes the immune system to attack certain joints that can result in discomfort and pain. Psoriatic Arthritis: This causes skin cells to multiply rapidly, which results in red and scaly patches on your skin called plaques. Multiple Sclerosis: MS tends to damage the protective coating that surrounds nerve cells (known as myelin sheath) and affects the transmission of neural messages between the brain and body. This leads to weakness, balance issues, along with other symptoms. Inflammatory Bowel Syndromes: This disease causes irritation of the intestinal lining. Graves' Disease: This disease attacks the thyroid gland in your neck and causes it to overproduce hormones, which results in an imbalance. Cancer: Cancerous tumors tend to secret substances that attract cytokines and free radicals that cause inflammation, which can lead to tumors growing.

If you already suffer from inflammation, it could make the situation words. Alzheimer's: The brain does not have pain receptors, but that doesn't mean it will not be able to feel the effects of inflammation. Researchers have recently discovered that people with a high level of Omega-6 fatty acids tend to have a greater chance of developing Alzheimer's. Different symptoms of Inflammation While there are different types of diseases that are caused by Inflammation, the early symptoms of them are similar. These include: Fatigue Muscle ache Low-grade fever Redness and swelling Numbness in your feet and hands Loss of hair Skin rash These are often accompanied by the symptoms that are specific to any disease the patient might be suffering from.

About Anti-Inflammatory Diet, generally speaking, an anti-inflammatory diet consists of a diet comprised of foods targeted towards the reduction of the uncontrolled inflammatory response in the body. The anti-inflammatory diet is rich in foods packed with anti-oxidants that are reactive molecules in the food to help to reduce free radicals, which causes cell damage to the body. There are many popular diets already following the anti-inflammatory principle, such as the Mediterranean diet, which is comprised of fish, good fats, and whole grains.

CHAPTER 9. FOODS GOOD FOR ANTI-INFLAMMATORY DIET

Despite popular belief, following an anti-inflammatory diet, isn't challenging. The following foods will encourage a healthy anti-inflammatory lifestyle: dark leafy greens such as kale and spinach blueberries, cherries, blackberries dark red grapes cauliflower and broccoli green tea beans and lentils red wine (in moderation) avocado and coconut olives extra virgin olive oil walnuts, almonds, pistachio, pine nuts cold-water fish; salmon and sardines spices and herbs; cinnamon , turmeric dark chocolate watermelon onion whole grains; brown rice, bulgur, quinoa eggs tomatoes.

These are just the basics; there is a lot more to look out for.

Foods Bad for Anti-Inflammatory Diet Foods you should avoid if you want to keep your inflammation in check. Sugary foods; soda, baked sweets, candy, sweetened coffee Vegetable oil products; mayonnaise, BBQ sauce, potato chips, crackers Fried foods; French fries, fish sticks, fried chicken, onion rings Refined flour products; pizza, pasta, flour tortillas, bagels, crackers Dairy; milk, yogurt, butter, soft cheeses Artificial sweeteners; means no-sugar-added products such as diet coke Artificial additives; including breakfast cereals, ice cream, candy Saturated fats; burgers, chips, pizza, and candy Conventional grain-fed meats; beef, pork, chicken Processed meats; bacon, sausage, jerky, hot dogs Gluten from store-bought products; bread, white flour Alcohol in excess Trans food fats; margarine, baked goods such as cookies, doughnuts, muffins Fast food.

Frequently Asked Questions

1. Should I Detox Before Anti-Inflammation? When you are detoxing your body, you are essentially flushing out the harmful toxins that have accumulated in your body. Completing a detox before embarking on your anti-inflammation is an excellent way of ensuring the effectiveness of your new lifestyle.

2. Should I See A Doctor for My Inflammation? An anti-inflammation lifestyle is a regime largely based on vegetables and requires an individual to omit certain products such as dairy products and red meat. If you are already following a similar kind of diet, such as vegan, then you would have fewer issues changing your eating habits. However, if you are taking such a step for the first time and trying to completely shift your lifestyle, it is recommended you consult a physician to ascertain you are in a healthy place to change your eating habits. Alternatively, if you are already suffering from an auto-immune disease, then it is even more advisable to consult with your doctor in order to create a meal plan according to your requirements.

3. Should I Exercise More? Having a fit and healthy body definitely helps reduce the possibility of experiencing issues when you begin this new lifestyle. If you are obese, you may face some inflammatory reactions, so it is better to start with a minimum level of exercise in your day-to-day routine before progressing to more strenuous exercising.

CHAPTER 10. TIPS ON TRANSITIONING TO AN ANTI-INFLAMMATORY LIFESTYLE

When you transition to the anti-inflammatory diet, you will need the inspiration to keep going when the tough times come! When you want that ice cream or that bag of crispy chips, but you know you are focusing on being healthy, the tips in this chapter will help you maintain your new healthy lifestyle and conquer those cravings that you are having.

The first tip to keep in mind is to have an anti-inflammatory vision board with a pictorial representation of your goals for going on the anti-inflammatory diet. You can use magazines, newspapers, or coupons, or a simple hand-drawn explanation to keep your goals right in front of you. During a moment of weakness, a quick glance to your board may be the trick to help you keep going. You could also use social media to pinpoint your favorite anti-inflammatory practitioners and blogs that you can check out when you want inspiration.

You will also want to consider keeping a food journal. It is a cool way to track your progress and to celebrate your victories. You can get an old notepad or a journal and keep daily track of what you ate during the day, making notes if you had any cravings, and did you give in or how did you handle it? A food journal will help you note patterns in your diet and what works for you and what doesn't in order to help you maintain the anti-inflammatory lifestyle as successfully as possible.

Make a personal goal to share your journey with someone else. Sharing your journey with others can add more meaning to it, and it can help others see the benefits of living an anti-inflammatory lifestyle.

As you transition, remember to take baby steps. You did not get chronic inflammation overnight, so you should also not expect it to heal overnight. Do not expect to lose 50 pounds in one week. Keep your goals realistic and celebrate your small successes.

Remember, this is not a diet, this is a lifestyle. As long as you are staying true to the lifestyle, the results should come. Remember to keep going, do not stop, and let the diet do the work for you.

Think about why you are eating or snacking? This may help you stop eating things that aren't good for you.

If you make a mistake, do not get discouraged. Tomorrow is a new day. Treat it like that and get back on your anti-inflammatory horse and ride it.

Host a dinner party! This will help others see what you are doing and help you on your journey.

Learn the anti-inflammatory equivalent of your favorite recipes from your desserts to your favorite pasta. Also, look for healthy substitutions of what you like.

A serving is equal to one cup of raw food or half a cup when it is cooked. A great rule of thumb is to try and eat 9 servings of fruits and vegetables every day.

Try at least one recipe or one new spice a week. This will help keep your journey fresh and fun. Also, never stop learning. Keep researching and learning about the anti-inflammatory diet so you can keep getting great results.

If you like to snack, try to eat at least 2 snacks daily. You can take anti-inflammatory supplements like fish oil or curcumin at that time as well.

Be prepared! Try to pre-cook your meals, so when you are feeling hungry you will not slide since you already have food prepared. You can also keep little snacks in places that you always visit so you have access to easy snacks.

If you do not like something or a tip doesn't work for you, do not feel guilty for not doing it. An anti-inflammatory diet is one that you can modify and you can adjust to your liking.

Get into the habits of reading ingredient lists. This can help you spot inflammatory ingredients that you didn't know where there. You can also double-check your sauces and condiments as well to see if they are causing inflammation or not.

Drink water! Drinking lots of water help you stay hydrated and can be extremely helpful.

Lastly, eat as many vegetables and healthy anti-inflammatory foods as you can? When was the last time you heard someone say that they got sick from eating so many vegetables?

Chapter 11: Breakfast

No Cook Overnight Oats
Preparation Time: 5 minsServings: 1
Ingredients:
1 ½ c. low fat milk
5 whole almond pieces
1 tsp. chia seeds
2 tbsps. Oats
1 tsp. sunflower seeds
1 tbsp. Craisins
Directions:
In a jar or mason bottle with cap, mix all ingredients.
Refrigerate overnight.
Enjoy for breakfast. Will keep in the fridge for up to 3 days.
Nutrition:
Calories: 271, Fat:9.8 g, Carbs:35.4 g, Protein:16.7 g, Sugars:9 g, Sodium:97 mg

Avocado Cup with Egg
Preparation Time: 5 minsServings: 4
Ingredients:
4 tsps. parmesan cheese
1 chopped stalk scallion
4 dashes pepper
4 dashes paprika
2 ripe avocados
4 medium eggs
Directions:
Preheat oven to 375 0F.
Slice avocadoes in half and discard the seed.
Slice the rounded portions of the avocado, to make it level and sit well on a baking sheet.
Place avocadoes on the baking sheet and crack one egg in each hole of the avocado.
Season each egg evenly with pepper, and paprika.
Pop in the oven and bake for 25 minutes or until eggs are cooked to your liking.
Serve with a sprinkle of parmesan.
Nutrition:
Calories: 206, Fat:15.4 g, Carbs:11.3 g, Protein:8.5 g, Sugars:0.4 g, Sodium:380 mg

Mediterranean Toast

Preparation Time: 10 mins Servings: 2

Ingredients:
- 1 ½ tsp. reduced-fat crumbled feta
- 3 sliced Greek olives
- ¼ mashed avocado
- 1 slice good whole wheat bread
- 1 tbsp. roasted red pepper hummus
- 3 sliced cherry tomatoes
- 1 sliced hardboiled egg

Directions:

First, toast the bread and top it with ¼ mashed avocado and 1 tablespoon hummus.

Add the cherry tomatoes, olives, hardboiled egg, and feta.

To taste, season with salt and pepper.

Nutrition:

Calories: 333.7, Fat:17 g, Carbs:33.3 g, Protein:16.3 g, Sugars:1 g, Sodium:700 mg

Instant Banana Oatmeal

Preparation Time: 1 Minute Servings: 1

Ingredients:
- 1 mashed ripe banana
- ½ c. water
- ½ c. quick oats

Directions:

Measure the oats and water into a microwave-safe bowl and stir to combine.

Place bowl in microwave and heat on high for 2 minutes.

Remove bowl from microwave and stir in the mashed banana and enjoy it.

Nutrition:

Calories: 243, Fat:3 g, Carbs:50 g, Protein:6 g, Sugars:20 g, Sodium:30 mg

Almond Butter-Banana Smoothie

Preparation Time: 5 mins Servings: 1

Ingredients:
- 1 tbsp. almond butter
- ½ c. ice cubes
- ½ c. packed spinach
- 1 peeled and frozen medium banana
- 1 c. fat-free milk

Directions:

In a powerful blender, blend all ingredients until smooth and creamy.

Serve and enjoy.

Nutrition:

Calories: 293, Fat:9.8 g, Carbs:42.5 g, Protein:13.5 g, Sugars:12 g, Sodium:111 mg

Brown Sugar Cinnamon Oatmeal

Preparation Time: 1 MinuteServings: 4
Ingredients:
½ tsp. ground cinnamon
1 ½ tsps. pure vanilla extract
¼ c. light brown sugar
2 c. low-fat milk
1 1/3 c. quick oats
Directions:
Measure the milk and vanilla into a medium saucepan and bring to a boil over medium-high heat.
Once boiling, reduce heat to medium. Stir in oats, brown sugar, and cinnamon, and cook, stirring, 2–3 minutes.
Serve immediately, sprinkled with additional cinnamon if desired.
Nutrition:
Calories: 208, Fat:3 g, Carbs:38 g, Protein:8 g, Sugars:15 g, Sodium:105 mg

Buckwheat Pancakes with Vanilla Almond Milk

Preparation Time: 10 minsServings: 1
Ingredients:
½ c. unsweetened vanilla almond milk
2-4 packets natural sweetener
1/8 tsp. salt
½ cup buckwheat flour
½ tsp. double-acting baking powder
Directions:
Prepare a nonstick pancake griddle and spray with the cooking spray, place over medium heat.
Whisk together the buckwheat flour, salt, baking powder, and stevia in a small bowl and stir in the almond milk after.
Onto the pan, scoop a large spoonful of batter, cook until bubbles no longer pop on the surface and the entire surface looks dry and (2-4 minutes). Flip and cook for another 2-4 minutes. Repeat with all the remaining batter.
Nutrition:
Calories: 240, Fat:4.5 g, Carbs:2 g, Protein:11 g, Sugars:17 g, Sodium:67 mg

Tomato Bruschetta with Basil

Preparation Time: 10 mins Servings: 8

Ingredients:
- ½ c. chopped basil
- 2 minced garlic cloves
- 1 tbsp. balsamic vinegar
- 2 tbsps. Olive oil
- ½ tsp. cracked black pepper
- 1 sliced whole wheat baguette
- 8 diced ripe Roma tomatoes
- 1 tsp. sea salt

Directions:

First, preheat the oven to 375 F.

In a bowl, dice the tomatoes, mix in balsamic vinegar, chopped basil, garlic, salt, pepper, and olive oil, set aside.

Slice the baguette into 16-18 slices and for about 10 minutes, place on a baking pan to bake. Serve with warm bread slices and enjoy.

For leftovers, store in an airtight container and put in the fridge. Try putting them over grilled chicken, it is amazing!

Nutrition:
Calories: 57, Fat:2.5 g, Carbs:7.9 g, Protein:1.4 g, Sugars:0.2 g, Sodium:261 mg

Sweet Corn Muffins

Preparation Time: 5 mins Servings: 1

Ingredients:
- 1 tbsp. sodium-free baking powder
- ¾ c. nondairy milk
- 1 tsp. pure vanilla extract
- ½ c. sugar
- 1 c. white whole-wheat flour
- 1 c. cornmeal
- ½ c. canola oil

Directions:

Preheat the oven to 400°F. Line a 12-muffin tin with paper liners and set aside.

Place the cornmeal, flour, sugar, and baking powder into a mixing bowl and whisk well to combine.

Add the nondairy milk, oil, and vanilla and stir just until combined.

Divide the batter evenly between the muffin cups. Place muffin tin on middle rack in the oven and bake for 15 minutes.

Remove from oven and place on a wire rack to cool.

Nutrition:
Calories: 203, Fat:9 g, Carbs:26 g, Protein:3 g, Sugars:9.5 g, Sodium:255 mg

SCRAMBLED EGGS WITH MUSHROOMS AND SPINACH

Preparation Time: 5 minsServings: 1

Ingredients:

2 egg whites
1 slice whole wheat toast
½ c. sliced fresh mushrooms
2 tbsps. Shredded fat-free American cheese
Pepper
1 tsp. olive oil
1 c. chopped fresh spinach
1 whole egg

Directions:

On medium-high fire, place a nonstick fry pan and add oil. Swirl oil to cover pan and heat for a minute.

Add spinach and mushrooms. Sauté until spinach is wilted, around 2-3 minutes.

Meanwhile, in a bowl whisk well egg, egg whites, and cheese. Season with pepper.

Pour egg mixture into pan and scramble until eggs are cooked through, around 3-4 minutes.

Serve and enjoy with a piece of whole wheat toast.

Nutrition:

Calories: 290.6, Fat:11.8 g, Carbs:21.8 g, Protein:24.3 g, Sugars:1.4 g, Sodium:1000 mg

CHIA AND OAT BREAKFAST BRAN

Preparation Time: overnight | Servings: 2

Ingredients:

85 g chopped roasted almonds
340 g coconut milk
30 g cane sugar
2½ g orange zest
30 g flax seed mix
170 g rolled oats
340 g blueberries
30 g chia seeds
2½ g cinnamon

Directions:

Add all your wet ingredients together and mix the sugar and milk in with the orange zest. Stir in the cinnamon and mix well. Once you are sure the sugar isn't lumpy add in the rolled oats, flax seeds, and chia and then let it sit for a minute.

Grab two bowls or mason jars and pour the mixture in. Top with the roasted almonds, and store in the fridge.

Pull it out in the morning and dig in!

Nutrition:

Calories: 353, Fat:8 g, Carbs:55 g, Protein:15 g, Sugars:9.9 g, Sodium:96 mg

Faux Breakfast Hash Brown Cups

Preparation Time: 15 minsServings: 8

Ingredients:

40 g diced onion
8 large eggs
7 ½ g garlic powder
2 ½ g pepper
170 g shredded low-fat cheese
170 g grated sweet potato
2 ½ g salt

Directions:

Preheat oven to 400 0F and prepare a muffin tin with liners.

Place grated sweet potatoes, onions, garlic, and spices into a bowl and mix well, before placing one spoonful in each cup. Add one large egg upon each cup and proceed to bake for 15 minutes until eggs are cooked.

Serve fresh or store.

Nutrition:

Calories: 143, Fat:9.1 g, Carbs:6 g, Protein:9 g, Sugars:0 g, Sodium:290 mg

Maple Mocha Frappe

Preparation Time: 2 minsServings: 2

Ingredients:

1 tbsp. unsweetened cocoa powder
½ c. low-fat milk
2 tbsps. Pure maple syrup
½ c. brewed coffee
1 small ripe banana
1 c. low-fat vanilla yogurt

Directions:

Place the banana in a blender or food processor and purée.

Add the remaining ingredients and pulse until smooth and creamy.

Serve immediately.

Nutrition:

Calories: 206, Fat:2 g, Carbs:38 g, Protein:6 g, Sugars:17 g, Sodium:65 mg

BREAKFAST OATMEAL IN SLOW COOKER

Preparation Time: 10 mins Servings: 8
Ingredients:
4 c. almond milk
2 packets stevia
2 c. steel-cut oats
1/3 c. chopped dried apricots
4 c. water
1/3 c. dried cherries
1 tsp. cinnamon
1/3 c. raisins

Directions:
In a slow cooker, mix well all ingredients.
Cover and set to low.
Cook for 8 hours.
You can set this the night before so that by morning you have breakfast ready.

Nutrition:
Calories: 158.5, Fat:2.9 g, Carbs:28.3 g, Protein:4.8 g, Sugars:11 g, Sodium:135 mg

APPLE CINNAMON OVERNIGHT OATS

Preparation Time: 15 mins Servings: 2
Ingredients:
1 diced apple
2 tbsps. Chia seeds
½ tbsp. ground cinnamon
½ tsp. pure vanilla extract
1¼ c. nonfat milk
Kosher salt
1 c. old-fashioned rolled oats
2 tsps. Honey

Directions:
Divide the oats, chia seeds or ground flaxseed, milk, cinnamon, honey or maple syrup, vanilla extract, and salt into two Mason jars. Place the lids tightly on top and shake until thoroughly combined.
Remove the lids and add half of the diced apple to each jar. Sprinkle with additional cinnamon, if desired. Place the lids tightly back on the jars and refrigerate for at least 4 hours or overnight.
You can store the overnight oats in single-serve containers in the refrigerator for up to 3 days.

Nutrition:
Calories: 339, Fat:8 g, Carbs:60 g, Protein:13 g, Sugars:15 g, Sodium:161 mg.

SPINACH MUSHROOM OMELETTE

Preparation Time: 5 minsServings: 2
Ingredients:
2 tbsps. Olive oil
2 whole eggs
3 c. spinach, fresh
Cooking spray
10 sliced baby Bella mushrooms
8 tbsps. Sliced red onion
4 egg whites
2 oz. goat cheese
Directions:
Place a skillet over medium-high heat and add olive.
Add the sliced red onions to the pan and stir until translucent. Then, add your mushrooms to the pan and keep stirring until they are slightly brown.
Add spinach and stir until they wilted. Season with a tiny bit of pepper and salt. Remove from heat.
Spray a small pan with cooking spray and Place over medium heat.
Break 2 whole eggs in a small bowl. Add 4 egg whites and whisk to combine.
Pour the whisked eggs into the small skillet and allow the mixture to sit for a minute.
Use a spatula to gently work your way around the skillet's edges. Raise the skillet and tip it down and around in a circular style to allow the runny eggs to reach the center and cook around the edges of the skillet.
Add crumbled goat cheese to a side of the omelet top with your mushroom mixture.
Then, gently fold the other side of the omelet over the mushroom side with the spatula.
Allowing cooking for thirty seconds. Then, transfer the omelet to a plate.
Nutrition:
Calories: 412, Fat:29 g, Carbs:18 g, Protein:25 g, Sugars:7 g, Sodium:1000 mg

Breakfast Grains and Fruits

Preparation Time: 10 mins Servings: 6

Ingredients:
1 c. raisins
¾ c. quick cooking brown rice
1 granny smith apple
1 orange
8 oz. low fat vanilla yogurt
3 c. water
¾ c. bulgur
1 red delicious apple

Directions:
On high fire, place a large pot and bring water to a boil.
Add bulgur and rice. Lower fire to a simmer and cook for ten minutes while covered.
Turn off fire, set aside for 2 minutes while covered.
In a baking sheet, transfer and evenly spread grains to cool.
Meanwhile, peel oranges and cut into sections. Chop and core apples.
Once grains are cool, transfer to a large serving bowl along with fruits.
Add yogurt and mix well to coat.
Serve and enjoy.

Nutrition:
Calories: 121, Fat:1 g, Carbs:24.2 g, Protein:3.8 g, Sugars:4.2 g, Sodium:500 mg

Eggs with Cheese

Preparation Time: 5 mins Servings: 1

Ingredients:
¼ c. chopped tomato
1 egg white
1 chopped green onion
2 tbsps. Fat-free milk
1 slice whole wheat bread
1 egg
½ oz. reduced fat grated cheddar cheese

Directions:
Mix the egg and egg whites in a bowl and add the milk.
Scramble the mixture in a non-stick frying pan until the eggs cook.
Meanwhile, toast the bread.
Spoon the scrambled egg mixture onto the toasted bread and top with the cheese until it melts.
Add the onion and the tomato.

Nutrition:
Calories: 251, Fat:11.0 g, Carbs:22.3 g, Protein:16.9 g, Sugars:1.8 g, Sodium:451 mg

Hearty Orange Peach Smoothie

Preparation Time: 5 minsServings: 2

Ingredients:

2 c. chopped peaches

2 tbsps. Unsweetened yogurt

Juice of 2 oranges

Directions:

Start by removing the seeds and peel from the peaches. Chop and leave some chunks of peach for topping.

Place the chopped peach, orange juice and yogurt in a blender and run until smooth.

You may add some water to thin the smoothie if you want.

Pour into glass cups and enjoy!

Nutrition:

Calories: 170, Fat:4.5 g, Carbs:28 g, Protein:7 g, Sugars:23 g, Sodium:101 mg

Cheddar & Kale Frittata

Preparation Time: 10 minsServings: 6

Ingredients:

1/3 c. sliced scallions

¼ tsp. pepper

1 diced red pepper

¾ c. non-fat milk

1 c. shredded sharp low-fat cheddar cheese

1 tsp. olive oil

5 oz. baby kale and spinach

12 eggs

Directions:

Preheat oven to 375 0F.

With olive oil, grease a glass casserole dish.

In a bowl, whisk well all ingredients except for cheese.

Pour egg mixture in prepared dish and bake for 35 minutes.

Remove from oven and sprinkle cheese on top and broil for 5 minutes.

Remove from oven and let it sit for 10 minutes.

Cut up and enjoy.

Nutrition:

Calories: 198, Fat:11.0 g, Carbs:5.7 g, Protein:18.7 g, Sugars:1 g, Sodium:209 mg.

Spinach and Tomato Egg Scramble

Preparation Time: 5 mins Servings: 1
Ingredients:
1 tsp. olive oil
1 tsp. chopped fresh basil
1 medium chopped tomato
¼ c. Swiss cheese
2 eggs
½ tsp. cayenne pepper
½ c. chopped packed spinach
Directions:
In a small bowl, whisk well eggs, basil, pepper, and Swiss cheese.
Place a medium fry pan on medium fire and heat oil.
Stir in tomato and sauté for 3 minutes. Stir in spinach and cook for 2 minutes or until starting to wilt.
Pour in beaten eggs and scramble for 2 to 3 minutes or to desired doneness.
Enjoy.
Nutrition:
Calories: 230, Fat:14.3 g, Carbs:8.4 g, Protein:17.9 g, Sugars:1 g, Sodium:247 mg.

French Toast with Cinnamon Vanilla

Preparation Time: 5 mins Servings: 4
Ingredients:
½ tsp. cinnamon
3 large eggs
1 tsp. vanilla
8 whole-wheat slices bread
2 tbsps. Low-fat milk
Directions:
First, preheat a griddle to 3500F.
Combine the vanilla, eggs, milk, and cinnamon in a small bowl and whisk until smooth. Pour into a plate or flat-bottomed dish.
Into the egg mixture, dip the bread, flip to coat both sides and put on the hot griddle.
Cook for about 2 minutes or until the bottom is lightly browned, then flip and cook the other side as well.
Nutrition:
Calories: 281.0, Fat:10.8 g, Carbs:37.2 g, Protein:14.5 g, Sugars:10 g, Sodium:390 mg.

Mango and Coconut Oatmeal

Preparation Time: 10 mins Servings: 1

Ingredients:

½ c. coconut milk

Kosher salt

1 c. old-fashioned rolled oats

1/3 c. fresh chopped mango

2 tbsps. Unsweetened coconut flakes

Directions:

Bring the milk to a boil in a medium saucepan over high heat. Stir in the oats and salt and reduce the heat to low. Simmer for about 5 minutes, until the oats are creamy and tender. In the meantime, toast coconut flakes for about 2 - 3 minutes until golden in a small dry skillet over low heat.

Once done, top the oatmeal with mango and coconut flakes, serve, and enjoy.

Nutrition:

Calories: 428, Fat:18 g, Carbs:60 g, Protein:10 g, Sugars:26 g, Sodium:122 mg.

Hot Honey Porridge

Preparation Time: 5 mins Servings: 4

Ingredients:

¼ c. honey

½ c. rolled oats

3 c. boiling water

¾ c. bulgur wheat

Directions:

Place the bulgur wheat and rolled oats into a saucepan. Add the boiling water and stir to combine.

Place pan over high heat and bring to a boil. Once boiling, reduce heat to low, then cover and simmer for 10 minutes, stirring occasionally.

Remove from heat, stir in honey, and serve immediately.

Nutrition:

Calories: 172, Fat:1 g, Carbs:40 g, Protein:4 g, Sugars:5 g, Sodium:20 mg

Chapter 12. Sides

Cauliflower and Potato Mash

Preparation Time: 5 mins Servings: 4
Ingredients:
½ tsp. flavored vinegar
1 minced garlic clove
2 lbs. Sliced potatoes
1 ½ c. water
8 oz. cauliflower florets
Directions:
Add water to your Instant Pot
Add potatoes and sprinkle cauliflower florets on top
Lock up the lid and cook on HIGH pressure for 5 minutes
Release the pressure naturally over 10 minutes
Sprinkle a bit of flavored vinegar and garlic
Mash and serve!
Nutrition:
Calories: 249, Fat:0.6 g, Carbs:55 g, Protein:7.5 g, Sugars:0.3 g, Sodium:56.3 mg

Grilled Asparagus

Preparation Time: 5 mins Servings: 6
Ingredients:
¼ tsp. garlic powder
1 tbsp. olive oil
¼ tsp. salt
2 bunches trimmed asparagus
1 tsp. lemon zest
Directions:
Preheat the grill to 375 – 400F.
Add the trimmed asparagus spears to a baking sheet.
Drizzle the asparagus with olive oil, garlic powder and salt, and using clean hands toss the asparagus well to coat with the seasoning.
Place the asparagus directly onto the grill grates and grill for 3-4 minutes, until slightly caramelized.
Remove from the grill and season with the, fresh lemon zest, and serve.
Nutrition:
Calories: 45, Fat:2 g, Carbs:6 g, Protein:3 g, Sugars:1.2 g, Sodium:74 mg

GARLIC STEAMED SQUASH

Preparation Time: 5 minsServings: 4

Ingredients:

2 small zucchinis
Freshly ground black pepper
All-purpose salt-free seasoning
2 medium yellow squash
6 peeled garlic cloves

Directions:

Trim the squash and zucchini and cut into 1-inch rounds.

Fill a steamer pot about 1 inch deep with water. Place pot over high heat and bring to a boil. Place the veggies and garlic into the steamer basket. Place the steamer basket into the pot and cover tightly with lid. Steam for 10 minutes.

Remove pot from heat and carefully remove lid. Pluck garlic cloves from pot and gently mash with a fork.

Transfer the steamed veggies to a serving bowl, add the mashed garlic and toss gently to coat. Season to taste with all-purpose salt-free seasoning and freshly ground black pepper. Serve immediately.

Nutrition:

Calories: 38, Fat:0 g, Carbs:8 g, Protein:2 g, Sugars:2.1 g, Sodium:3.3 mg

SATISFYING CORN COB

Preparation Time: 5 minsServings: 8

Ingredients:

2 c. water
8 corn ears

Directions:

Husk the corns and cut the bottom part of the corns, wash them well thoroughly Wash well
Add water to the cooker base and arrange the corns vertically with the large part submerged underwater and the small part pointing upward
Lock up the lid and cook on HIGH pressure for 2 minutes
Release the pressure naturally
Serve with a bit of flavored vinegar and vegan butter

Nutrition:

Calories: 63, Fat:1 g, Carbs:14 g, Protein:2.4 g, Sugars:2.3 g, Sodium:2.5 mg

DEVILLED EGGS

Preparation Time: 10 minsServings: 12
Ingredients:
1/3 c. plain fat-free Greek yogurt
¼ tsp. ground black pepper
1 tsp. yellow mustard
1 tsp. white sugar
6 large eggs
¼ tsp. fine sea salt
1 tsp. red wine vinegar

Directions:
Put the eggs in a large, deep saucepan, and add enough water to completely cover them by ½ an inch.
Let the water boil, and then cook the eggs for 12 minutes.
Drain the hot water from the pan and cover the eggs in cold water. Rest the eggs rest for 2 minutes.
Drain the water and repeat this process until the eggs have completely cooled.
Peel the shell, and then halve each egg lengthwise.
Separate the yolks from the whites.
Use only 5 of the 6 egg yolks, and put them in a small bowl.
Using a fork, mash the yolks until there are no large lumps, and then add the mustard, Greek yogurt, sugar, vinegar, salt, and pepper to the bowl. Stir this mixture until all the ingredients are well combined and smooth.
You may transfer this filling to a small plastic food storage bag and snipping off one of the corners of the bag, make a piping bag or you may simply spoon the filling into the egg whites.
Squeeze the egg yolk filling through hole in the piping bag into the egg whites, and serve garnish with paprika or parsley leaves, if desired.

Nutrition:
Calories: 37, Fat:2.1 g, Carbs:0.8 g, Protein:3.8 g, Sugars:0.33 g, Sodium:94 mg

BORDERS APART MEXICAN CAULIFLOWER RICE

Preparation Time: 5 minsServings: 4
Ingredients:
4 tbsps. Tomato paste
1 ½ c. water
1 can fire roasted tomatoes
3 c. chopped onion
6 c. cooked brown rice
2 c. salsa
6 garlic cloves

Directions:
Add the listed ingredients to your Instant Pot
Lock up the lid and cook on HIGH pressure for 5 minutes
Release the pressure naturally
Stir in chopped cilantro and top up with your desired toppings
Enjoy!

Nutrition:
Calories: 562, Fat:25 g, Carbs:63 g, Protein:23 g, Sugars:5.8 g, Sodium:201.2 mg

Egg and Bean Medley

Preparation Time: 5 mins Servings: 3
Ingredients:
5 beaten eggs
1 tsp. chili powder
2 chopped garlic cloves
½ c. milk
½ c. tomato sauce
1 c. cooked white beans
Directions:
Add milk and eggs to a bowl and mix well
Add the rest of the ingredients and mix well
Add a cup of water to the pot
Transfer the bowl to your pot and lock up the lid
Cook on HIGH pressure for 18 minutes
Release the pressure naturally over 10 minutes
Serve with warm bread
Enjoy!
Nutrition:
Calories: 206, Fat:9 g, Carbs:23 g, Protein:9 g, Sugars:0.6 g, Sodium:917.2 mg

Cheddar and Apple Panini Sandwich

Preparation Time: 5 mins Servings: 2
Ingredients:
Cooking spray
½ c. arugula
4 whole-wheat bread slices
4 low-fat cheddar cheese slices
2 tbsps. low-fat honey mustard
1 thinly sliced apple
Directions:
Set Panini press on medium heat.
Spread the mustard on each slice of the bread. Lay the apple on two of the bread slices, top with cheese and then the arugula. Top with the other two slices of bread.
Coat the Panini press with cooking spray and grill each sandwich for 4-5 minutes.
Allow to cool before serving.
Nutrition:
Calories: 22, Fat:4 g, Carbs:23 g, Protein:11 g, Sugars:16 g, Sodium:570 mg

ROASTED CARROTS

Preparation Time: 15 mins Servings: 4

Ingredients:
2 lbs. peeled and halved carrots
½ tsp. sea salt
2 tbsps. olive oil
Flat leaf parsley
1 tbsp. raw honey
½ tsp. black pepper

Directions:
Preheat the oven to 400F.
Peel the carrots, cutting off the stems, and then cut the carrots in half creating a piece with a wide and narrow half.
Halve each carrot in half again lengthwise.
Place all the cut carrots into a bowl and add the olive oil, salt, pepper, and raw honey. Toss the carrots well to coat.
Spread the carrots evenly onto a baking sheet lined with aluminum foil, making sure they are all in a single layer.
Bake the carrots for 30 minutes, and then remove from oven to cool.
Garnish with fresh flat leaf parsley, if desired.

Nutrition:
Calories: 109, Fat:5.8 g, Carbs:14 g, Protein:1.4 g, Sugars:11 g, Sodium:264 mg

FANCY RED AND WHITE SPROUTS

Preparation Time: 10 mins Servings: 3

Ingredients:
¼ c. toasted pine nuts
½ tsp. flavored vinegar
1 grated pepper
1 lb. Brussels sprouts
1 pomegranate
1 tbsp. extra virgin olive oil

Directions:
Remove the outer leaves and trim the stems
Wash the Brussels
Cut the largest one in half and get all the ones in uniform size
Add 1 cup of water
Put steamer basket
Add sprouts to steamer basket
Lock up the lid and cook on HIGH pressure for 3 minutes
Release the pressure naturally
Move sprouts to serving dish and dress with olive oil, pepper and flavored vinegar
Sprinkle toasted pine nuts and pomegranate seeds
Serve and enjoy!

Nutrition:
Calories: 197, Fat:7 g, Carbs:22 g, Protein:6 g, Sugars:1.9 g, Sodium:22 mg

Garlic and Chive "Mash"

Preparation Time: 8 mins Servings: 5

Ingredients:
- 2 lbs. peeled Yukon potatoes
- 4 peeled garlic cloves
- ¼ c. chopped chives
- ½ tsp. flavored vinegar
- 2 c. vegetable stock
- ½ c. almond milk

Directions:
- Add broth, garlic and potatoes to the Instant Pot
- Lock up the lid and cook on HIGH pressure for 9 minutes
- Release the pressure naturally over 10 minutes
- Drain just the amount of liquid required to maintain your required consistency
- Mash the potatoes and stir in flavored vinegar and milk
- Stir in chives and serve
- Enjoy!

Nutrition:
Calories: 293, Fat:14 g, Carbs:35 g, Protein:8 g, Sugars:2.9 g, Sodium:313.7 mg

CRASHING ASPARAGUS RISOTTO WITH MICROSTOCK

Preparation Time: 10 mins Servings: 2

Ingredients:
- 2 c. Arborio rice
- 1 medium size chopped red onion
- ½ tsp. lemon juice
- 4 c. water
- 1 lb. asparagus
- 2 tbsps. Olive oil
- ¼ c. white wine vinegar
- 2 tsps. Flavored vinegar

Directions:
- Trim the asparagus by removing the stem, wash them under cold water and slice them in rondels making sure to keep the tips
- Add woody stems and water to your Instant Pot
- Lock up the lid and cook on HIGH pressure for 12 minutes, release the pressure naturally
- Lift out the woody stem and discard the cooking liquid
- Pour the liquid into a measuring cup
- Add onion, olive oil to the pot and swirl
- Add rice, onion and stir
- Cook for 2 minutes
- Splash in a bit of wine vinegar and deglaze
- Add asparagus micro stock, asparagus rondels and tips
- Season with flavored vinegar
- Lock up the lid and cook on HIGH pressure for 6 minutes
- Release the pressure naturally
- Add a squeeze of lemon juice and serve
- Enjoy!

Nutrition:
Calories: 486, Fat:7 g, Carbs:71 g, Protein:37 g, Sugars:0 g, Sodium:700.6 mg

TURKEY AND MELTED CHEESE SANDWICH

Preparation Time: 10 mins Servings: 2

Ingredients:
- 2 tsps. Dijon mustard
- ½ c. thinly sliced cucumber
- 2 whole-grain bread slices
- 2 low-sodium smoked turkey slices
- Pepper.
- ¼ c. shredded low-fat mozzarella

Directions:
- Spread the mustard on each of the slices.
- Lay the smoked turkey slice and then the cucumber slices on top of the bread. Sprinkle with the mozzarella and season with pepper.
- Toaster to melt the cheese for about 3 minutes.
- Serve while warm.

Nutrition:
Calories: 380, Fat:13.5 g, Carbs:40 g, Protein:25 g, Sugars:2.41 g, Sodium:550 mg

GARLIC AND BROCCOLI MISHMASH
Preparation Time: 3 minsServings: 4
Ingredients:
6 minced garlic cloves
½ c. water
White wine vinegar
Sea flavored vinegar
2 broccoli head cut up into florets
1 tbsp. peanut oil
Directions:
Place a steamer rack in your cooker
Add the florets to the rack
Add ½ a cup of water to the pot
Lock up the lid and cook on LOW pressure for 0 minutes
Quick release
Allow the broccoli to cool by transferring them to an ice bath
Remove water and set the pot to Sauté mode
Add 1 tablespoon of peanut oil alongside minced garlic
Sauté for 25-30 seconds and add the broccoli alongside 1 tablespoon of white wine vinegar
Season with a bit of flavored vinegar and stir for 30 seconds
Enjoy!
Nutrition:
Calories: 101, Fat:8 g, Carbs:6 g, Protein:6 g, Sugars:0.2 g, Sodium:41.5 mg

CRUNCHY CREAMY MASHED SWEET POTATOES
Preparation Time: 5 minsServings: 4
Ingredients:
¼ tsp. nutmeg
1 c. water
2 lbs. Sliced garnet sweet potatoes
Sea flavored vinegar
2 tbsps. Maple syrup
3 tbsps. Vegan butter
Directions:
Peel the sweet potatoes and cut up into 1inch chunks
Pour 1 cup of water to the pot and add steamer basket
Add sweet potato chunks in the basket
Lock up the lid and cook on HIGH pressure for 8 minutes
Quick release the pressure
Open the lid and place the cooked sweet potatoes to the bowl
Use a masher to mash the potatoes
Add ¼ teaspoon of nutmeg, 2-3 tablespoons of unflavored vinegar butter, 2 tablespoon of maple syrup
Mash and mix
Season with flavored vinegar
Serve and enjoy!
Nutrition:
Calories: 249, Fat:8 g, Carbs:37 g, Protein:7 g, Sugars:13.9 g, Sodium:200 mg

Ultimate Roast Potatoes

Preparation Time: 5 mins Servings: 4

Ingredients:
- Pepper
- 2 lbs. baby potatoes
- 3 skinned out garlic clove
- ½ c. stock
- 5 tbsps. Olive oil
- 1 rosemary sprig

Directions:
- Set your pot to Sauté mode and add oil
- Once it is heated up, add in the garlic, rosemary and potatoes
- Sauté the potatoes for 10 minutes and brown them
- Take a sharp knife and cut a small piece in the middle of your potatoes and pour the stock
- Lock up the lid and cook on HIGH pressure for 7 minutes
- Once done, wait for 10 minutes and release the pressure naturally
- Add garlic cloves and peel the potatoes skin
- Sprinkle a bit of pepper and enjoy!

Nutrition:
Calories: 42, Fat:1.3 g, Carbs:7.3 g, Protein:0.8 g, Sugars:1.7 g, Sodium:501 mg

Personal and Intimate Soy Milk

Preparation Time: 10 mins Servings: 2

Ingredients:
- 5 c. water
- 1 vanilla bean extract piece
- ¼ tsp. cinnamon
- ½ c. organic yellow soy bean
- ½ tsp. stevia

Directions:
- You need to soak the beans under water for about 36 hours prior to making the recipe
- Strain the beans and replace old water with new after every 12 hours
- Take a cutting board and chop up the soy beans
- Take a small sized bowl and add the chopped-up beans alongside ½ a cup of water
- Add the mix to your blender and puree for 90 seconds
- Pour the puree into your pot and add 5 cups of water
- Give it a nice stir
- Set your pot to Sauté mode and allow it to reach boiling point (foam will appear)
- Stir it well and lock up the lid. Cook for 9 minutes under HIGH pressure
- Allow the pressure to release naturally
- Take another bowl and add stevia, vanilla bean extract, cinnamon and mix well
- Open the lid and carefully strain the liquid into this bowl
- Give it a nice stir and your milk is ready!
- Enjoy

Nutrition:
Calories: 131, Fat:4.3 g, Carbs:15 g, Protein:23 g, Sugars:1 g, Sodium:81.9 mg

EXTREMELY CRAZY EGG DEVILS

Preparation Time: 5 mins Servings: 6

Ingredients:

Guacamole
Furikake
Mayonnaise
8 large eggs
1 c. water
Sliced radishes

Directions:

Add 1 cup of water to your Instant Pot
Place the steamer insert in your pot
Arrange the eggs on top of the insert
Lock up the lid and cook for about 6 minutes at HIGH pressure
Allow the pressure to release naturally
Transfer the eggs to an ice bath and peel the skin
Cut the eggs in half and garnish them with dressings of Guacamole, sliced up radishes, Mayonnaise, Furikake, Sliced up Parmesan etc.!

Nutrition:

Calories: 137, Fat:10 g, Carbs:1 g, Protein:11 g, Sugars:1 g, Sodium:265 mg

GREEN PEA PURÉE

Preparation Time: 20 mins Servings: 2

Ingredients:

2 boiled sliced carrots
¼ c. 20% fat sour cream
Pepper.
2 c. green peas
Salt.

Directions:

Boil the carrots and the peas.
Using a blender purée the vegetables. Season with salt and pepper. Top with sour cream.

Nutrition:

Calories: 101, Fat:2.1 g, Carbs:14 g, Protein:7 g, Sugars:2.8 g, Sodium:57.2 mg

Herbed Green Beans

Preparation Time: 5 mins Servings: 4

Ingredients:
- ½ c. chopped fresh mint
- 2 minced garlic cloves
- 1 tsp. lemon zest
- 4 c. trimmed green beans
- 1 tbsp. olive oil
- 1 tsp. coarse ground black pepper
- ½ c. chopped fresh parsley

Directions:

Heat the olive oil in a large sauté pan over medium heat. Add the green beans and garlic. Sauté until the green beans are crisp tender, approximately 5-6 minutes.

Add the mint, parsley, lemon zest, and black pepper. Toss to coat.

Serve immediately.

Nutrition:

Calories: 66.2, Fat:3.5 g, Carbs:8.3 g, Protein:2.1 g, Sugars:2 g, Sodium:65 mg

Easy Lemon Roasted Radishes

Preparation Time: 5 mins Servings: 2

Ingredients:
- 2 bunches rinsed and quartered radishes
- 2 tsps. Lemon juice
- Salt.
- 1½ tsp. roughly fresh chopped rosemary
- 1 tbsp. melted coconut oil
- Pepper

Directions:

Heat the oven to 350°F. Line a baking sheet with parchment paper.

Add pepper, salt, coconut oil, and radishes to a bowl and mix until combined.

Place the mixture on a baking sheet and bake for about 35 minutes, stirring occasionally.

When it is done, toss with rosemary and lemon juice.

Serve and enjoy.

Nutrition:

Calories: 37, Fat:2 g, Carbs:4 g, Protein:1 g, Sugars:2 g, Sodium:95 mg

Green Beans with Nuts

Preparation Time: 20 mins Servings: 2
Ingredients:
3 minced garlic cloves
1 tbsp. olive oil
½ c. chopped walnuts
2 c. sliced green beans
Directions:
Boil the beans in salted water until tender.
Place the beans, garlic and walnuts in a preheated pan and cook for about 5-7 minutes on the stove.
Nutrition:
Calories: 285, Fat:24.1 g, Carbs:7.1 g, Protein:10 g, Sugars:3.3 g, Sodium:311 mg

Beets Stewed with Apples

Preparation Time: 1 hour | Servings: 2
Ingredients:
2 tbsps. Tomato paste
1 tbsps. Olive oil
1 c. water
2 peeled, cored and sliced apples
3 peeled, boiled and grated beets
2 tbsps. Sour cream
Directions:
Boil the beets until half-done
In a deep pan preheated with olive oil cook the grated beets for 15 minutes.
Add the sliced apples, tomato paste, sour cream and 1 cup water. Stew for 30 minutes covered.
Nutrition:
Calories: 346, Fat:7.7 g, Carbs:26.8 g, Protein:2 g, Sugars:10.2 g, Sodium:96.1 mg

Cabbage Quiche

Preparation Time: 30 mins Servings: 4

Ingredients:
- 2 beaten eggs
- 2 tbsps. Sour cream
- 2 tsps. Semolina
- Fresh parsley
- ½ shredded white cabbage head
- 2 tbsps. milk
- Salt

Directions:

In a saucepan stew the shredded cabbage with milk until soft and done.

Sprinkle the semolina over the cabbage, constantly stirring, and cook for 10 minutes more.

Remove from the heat, let cool and stir in the beaten eggs. Season with salt.

Arrange the cabbage mixture in a baking dish, coat with sour cream and bake at 400F for 20 minutes.

Serve with sour cream and fresh parsley leaves.

Nutrition:

Calories: 93, Fat:0.5 g, Carbs:27.8 g, Protein:19.4 g, Sugars:3.1 g, Sodium:561.6 mg

Baked Tomatoes

Preparation Time: 5 mins Servings: 2

Ingredients:
- 2 minced garlic cloves
- 2 tbsps. Olive oil
- 2 sliced large tomatoes
- 2 tbsps. Minced basil
- 1 minced rosemary sprig

Directions:

Brush a baking sheet with olive oil.

Arrange the tomato slices on the baking sheet. Sprinkle with garlic, basil and rosemary. Brush with olive oil.

Bake in a preheated 350°F oven for 5-10 minutes.

Nutrition:

Calories: 161, Fat:14.5 g, Carbs:2 g, Protein:0.4 g, Sugars:2 g, Sodium:4 mg

Chapter 13. Poultry

Chicken and Veggies

Preparation Time: 10 minsServings: 4
Ingredients:
½ c. chopped yellow onion
16 oz. cauliflower florets
2 tbsps. Organic olive oil
½ tsp. Italian seasoning
14 oz. chopped no-salt-added canned tomatoes
4 de-boned, skinless and cubed chicken breasts
¼ tsp. black pepper
Directions:
Heat up a pan while using the oil over medium-high heat, add chicken, black pepper, onion and Italian seasoning, toss and cook for 5 minutes.
Add tomatoes and cauliflower, toss, cover the pan and cook over medium heat for twenty possibly even minutes.
Toss again, divide everything between plates and serve.
Enjoy!
Nutrition:
Calories: 310, Fat:6 g, Carbs:14 g, Protein:20 g, Sugars:6 g, Sodium:550 mg

Hidden Valley Chicken Drummies

Preparation Time: 45 minsServings: 6 - 8
Ingredients:
2 tbsps. Hot sauce
½ c. melted butter
Celery sticks
2 packages Hidden Valley dressing dry mix
3 tbsps. Vinegar
12 chicken drumsticks
Paprika
Directions:
Preheat the oven to 350 0F.
Rinse and pat dry the chicken.
In a bowl blend the dry dressing, melted butter, vinegar and hot sauce. Stir until combined.
Place the drumsticks in a large plastic baggie, pour the sauce over drumsticks. Massage the sauce until the drumsticks are coated.
Place the chicken in a single layer on a baking dish. Sprinkle with paprika.
Bake for 30 minutes, flipping halfway.
Serve with crudité or salad.
Nutrition:
Calories: 155, Fat:18 g, Carbs:96 g, Protein:15 g, Sugars:0.7 g, Sodium:340 mg

Lemon-Parsley Chicken Breast

Preparation Time: 15 mins Servings: 2

Ingredients:

1/3 c. lemon juice
¼ c. fresh parsley
1/3 c. white wine
3 tbsps. Bread crumbs
2 skinless and boneless chicken breasts
2 minced garlic cloves
2 tbsps. Flavorless oil

Directions:

Combine the wine, lemon juice and garlic in a measuring cup.
Pound each chicken breast, until they are ¼ inch thick.
Coat the chicken with bread crumbs, and heat the oil in a large skillet.
Fry the chicken for 6 minutes on each side, until they turn brown.
Stir in the wine mixture over the chicken.
Simmer for 5 minutes
Serve. Pour any extra juices over the chicken. Garnish with parsley.

Nutrition:

Calories: 117, Fat:12 g, Carbs:74 g, Protein:14 g, Sugars:5.8 g, Sodium:0 mg

Chicken and Brussels sprouts

Preparation Time: 10 mins |Servings: 4

Ingredients:

1 cored, peeled and chopped apple
1 chopped yellow onion
1 tbsp. organic olive oil
3 c. shredded Brussels sprouts
1 lb. ground chicken meat
Black pepper

Directions:

Heat up a pan while using oil over medium-high heat, add chicken, stir and brown for 5 minutes.
Add Brussels sprouts, onion, black pepper and apple, stir, cook for 10 minutes, divide into bowls and serve.
Enjoy!

Nutrition:

Calories: 200, Fat:8 g, Carbs:13 g, Protein:9 g, Sugars:3.3 g, Sodium:194 mg

Chicken Divan

Preparation Time: 45 minutes | Servings: 4
Ingredients:
1 c. croutons
1 c. cooked and diced broccoli pieces
½ c. water
1 c. grated extra sharp cheddar cheese
½ lb. de-boned and skinless cooked chicken pieces
1 can mushroom soup
Directions:
Preheat the oven to 350 ° F
In a large pot, heat the soup and water. Add the chicken, broccoli, and cheese. Combine thoroughly.
Pour into a greased baking dish.
Place the croutons over the mixture.
Bake for 30 minutes or until the casserole is bubbling and the croutons are golden brown.
Nutrition:
Calories: 380, Fat:22 g, Carbs:10 g, Protein:25 g, Sugars:2 g, Sodium:475 mg

Spicy Pulled Chicken Wraps

Preparation Time: 15 minsServings: 6-8
Ingredients:
1 head romaine lettuce
1½ tsps. Ground cumin
1½ c. low-fat, low-sodium chicken broth
1 tsp. paprika
1 tsp. garlic powder
1 lb. skinless, de-boned chicken breasts
2 tsps. Chili powder
Directions:
In a slow cooker add all ingredients except lettuce and gently, stir to combine.
Set the slow cooker on low.
Cover and cook for about 6-8 hours.
Uncover the slow cooker and transfer the breasts into a large plate.
With a fork, shred the breasts.
Serve the shredded beef over lettuce leaves.
Nutrition:
Calories: 150, Fat:3.4 g, Carbs:12 g, Protein:14 g, Sugars:7 g, Sodium:900 mg

Apricot Chicken Wings

Preparation Time: 15 minsServings: 3 - 4

Ingredients:

1 medium jar apricot preserve
1 package Lipton onion dry soup mix
1 medium bottle Russian dressing
2 lbs. chicken wings

Directions:

Pre-heat the oven to 350 ° F.
Rinse and pat dry the chicken wings.
Place the chicken wings on a baking pan, single layer.
Bake for 45 – 60 minutes, turning halfway.
In a medium bowl, combine the Lipton soup mix, apricot preserve and Russian dressing.
Once the wings are cooked, toss with the sauce, until the pieces are coated.
Serve immediately with a side dish.

Nutrition:

Calories: 162, Fat:17 g, Carbs:76 g, Protein:13 g, Sugars:24 g, Sodium:700 mg

Chicken and Broccoli

Preparation Time: 10 minsServings: 4

Ingredients:

2 minced garlic cloves
4 de-boned, skinless chicken breasts
½ c. coconut cream
1 tbsp. chopped oregano
2 c. broccoli florets
1 tbsp. organic olive oil
1 c. chopped red onions

Directions:

Heat up a pan while using the oil over medium-high heat, add chicken breasts and cook for 5 minutes on each side.
Add onions and garlic, stir and cook for 5 minutes more.
Add oregano, broccoli and cream, toss everything, cook for ten minutes more, divide between plates and serve.
Enjoy!

Nutrition:

Calories: 287, Fat:10 g, Carbs:14 g, Protein:19 g, Sugars:10 g, Sodium:1106 mg

Balsamic Roast Chicken

Preparation Time: 10 mins Servings: 4

Ingredients:
- 1 tbsp. minced fresh rosemary
- 1 minced garlic clove
- Black pepper
- 1 tbsp. olive oil
- 1 tsp. brown sugar
- 6 rosemary sprigs
- 1 whole chicken
- ½ c. balsamic vinegar

Directions:

Combine garlic, minced rosemary, black pepper and the olive oil. Rub the chicken with the herbal olive oil mixture.

Put 3 rosemary sprigs into the chicken cavity.

Place the chicken into a roasting pan and roast at 400F for about 1 hr. 30 minutes.

When the chicken is golden and the juices run clear, transfer to a serving dish.

In a saucepan dissolve the sugar in balsamic vinegar over heat. Do not boil.

Carve the chicken and top with vinegar mixture.

Nutrition:

Calories: 587, Fat:37.8 g, Carbs:2.5 g, Protein:54.1 g, Sugars:0 g, Sodium:600 mg

Chicken, Bell Pepper & Spinach Frittata

Preparation Time: 15 mins Servings: 8

Ingredients:
- ¾ c. frozen chopped spinach
- ¼ tsp. garlic powder
- ¼ c. chopped red onion
- 1 1/3 c. finely chopped cooked chicken
- 8 eggs
- Freshly ground black pepper
- 1½ c. chopped and seeded red bell pepper

Directions:

Grease a large slow cooker.

In a bowl, add eggs, garlic powder and black pepper and beat well.

Place remaining ingredients into prepared slow cooker.

Pour egg mixture over chicken mixture and gently, stir to combine.

Cover and cook for about 2-3 hours.

Nutrition:

Calories: 250.9, Fat:16.3 g, Carbs:10.8 g, Protein:16.2 g, Sugars:4 g, Sodium:486 mg

Hot Chicken Wings

Preparation Time: 25 mins Servings: 4 - 5

Ingredients:

2 tbsps. Honey
½ stick margarine
2 tbsps. Cayenne pepper
1 bottle durkee hot sauce
10 - 20 chicken wings
10 shakes Tabasco sauce

Directions:

In a deep pot, heat the canola oil. Deep-fry the wings until cooked, approximately 20 minutes.
In a medium bowl, mix the hot sauce, honey, tabasco, and cayenne pepper. Mix well.
Place the cooked wings on paper towels. Drain the excess oil.
Toss the chicken wings in the sauce until coated evenly.

Nutrition:

Calories: 102, Fat:14 g, Carbs:55 g, Protein:23 g, Sugars:0.3 g, Sodium:340 mg

Balsamic Chicken and Beans

Preparation Time: 10 mins Servings: 4

Ingredients:

1 lb. trimmed fresh green beans
¼ c. balsamic vinegar
2 sliced shallots
2 tbsps. Red pepper flakes
4 skinless, de-boned chicken breasts
2 minced garlic cloves
3 tbsps. Extra virgin olive oil

Directions:

Combine 2 tablespoons of the olive oil with the balsamic vinegar, garlic, and shallots. Pour it over the chicken breasts and refrigerate overnight.
The next day, preheat the oven to 375 0F.
Take the chicken out of the marinade and arrange in a shallow baking pan. Discard the rest of the marinade.
Bake in the oven for 40 minutes.
While the chicken is cooking, bring a large pot of water to a boil.
Place the green beans in the water and allow them to cook for five minutes and then drain.
Heat one tablespoon of olive oil in the pot and return the green beans after rinsing them.
Toss with red pepper flakes.

Nutrition:

Calories: 433, Fat:17.4 g, Carbs:12.9 g, Protein:56.1 g, Sugars:13 g, Sodium:292 mg

BUTTER CHICKEN

Preparation Time: 10 minsServings: 6
Ingredients:
8 finely chopped garlic cloves
¼ c. chopped low-fat unsalted butter
Freshly ground black pepper
6 oz. skinless, de-boned chicken thighs
1 tsp. lemon pepper
Directions:
In a large slow cooker, place chicken thighs.
Top chicken thighs with butter evenly.
Sprinkle with garlic, lemon pepper and black pepper evenly.
Set the slow cooker on low.
Cover and cook for about 6 hours.
Nutrition:
Calories: 438, Fat:28 g, Carbs:14 g, Protein:30 g, Sugars:2 g, Sodium:700 mg

FIVE-SPICE ROASTED DUCK BREASTS

Preparation Time: 10 minsServings: 4
Ingredients:
1 tsp. five-spice powder
¼ tsp. cornstarch
2 orange juice and zest
1 tbsp. reduced-sodium soy sauce
2 lbs. de-boned duck breast
½ tsp. kosher salt
2 tsps. Honey
Directions:
Preheat oven to 375 0F.
Place duck skin-side down on a cutting board. Trim off all excess skin that hangs over the sides. Turnover and make three parallel, diagonal cuts in the skin of each breast, cutting through the fat but not into the meat. Sprinkle both sides with five-spice powder and salt.
Place the duck skin-side down in an ovenproof skillet over medium-low heat.
Cook until the fat is melted and the skin is golden brown, about 10 minutes. Transfer the duck to a plate; pour off all the fat from the pan. Return the duck to the pan skin-side up and transfer to the oven.
Roast the duck for 10 to 15 minutes for medium, depending on the size of the breast, until a thermometer inserted into the thickest part registers 150 0F.
Transfer to a cutting board; let rest for 5 minutes.
Pour off any fat remaining in the pan (take care, the handle will still be hot); place the pan over medium-high heat and add orange juice and honey. Bring to a simmer, stirring to scrape up any browned bits.
Add orange zest and soy sauce and continue to cook until the sauce is slightly reduced, about 1 minute. Stir cornstarch mixture then whisk into the sauce; cook, stirring, until slightly thickened, 1 minute.
Remove the duck skin and thinly slice the breast meat. Drizzle with the orange sauce.
Nutrition:
Calories: 152, Fat:2 g, Carbs:8 g, Protein:24 g, Sugars:5 g, Sodium:309 mg

Chicken and Radish Mix

Preparation Time: 10 minutes | Servings: 4
Ingredients:
10 halved radishes
1 tbsp. organic olive oil
2 tbsps. Chopped chives
1 c. low-sodium chicken stock
4 chicken things
Black pepper
Directions:
Heat up a pan with all the oil over medium-high heat, add chicken, season with black pepper and brown for 6 minutes on either side.
Add stock and radishes, reduce heat to medium and simmer for twenty minutes.
Add the chives, toss, divide between plates and serve.
Enjoy!
Nutrition:
Calories: 247, Fat:10 g, Carbs:12 g, Protein:22 g, Sugars:1.1 g, Sodium:673 mg

Chicken with Broccoli

Preparation Time: 15 minsServings: 4
Ingredients:
1 chopped small white onion
1½ c. low-fat, low-sodium chicken broth
Freshly ground black pepper
2 c. chopped broccoli
1 lb. cubed, skinless and de-boned chicken thighs
2 minced garlic cloves
Directions:
In a slow cooker, add all ingredients and mix well.
Set slow cooker on low.
Cover and cook for 4-5 hours.
Serve hot.
Nutrition:
Calories: 300, Fat:9 g, Carbs:19 g, Protein:31 g, Sugars:6 g, Sodium:200 mg

Chicken, Pasta and Snow Peas

Preparation Time: 20 mins Servings: 1 - 2

Ingredients:
Fresh ground pepper
2 ½ c. penne pasta
1 standard jar tomato and basil pasta sauce
1 c. halved and trimmed snow peas
1 lb. chicken breasts
1 tsp. olive oil

Directions:
In a medium frying pan, heat the olive oil. Season the chicken breasts with salt and pepper.
Cook the chicken breasts until cooked through for approximately 5 – 7 minutes each side.
Cook the pasta according to instructions on package. Cook the snow peas with the pasta.
Scoop 1 cup of the pasta water. Drain the pasta and peas, set aside.
Once the chicken is cooked, slice diagonally.
Add the chicken back to the frying pan. Add the pasta sauce. If the mixture seems dry.
Add some of the pasta water to desired consistency. Heat together.
Divide into bowls and serve immediately.

Nutrition:
Calories: 140, Fat:17 g, Carbs:52 g, Protein:34 g, Sugars:2.3 g, Sodium:400 mg

Roast Chicken Dal

Preparation Time: 10 mins Servings: 4

Ingredients:
15 oz. rinsed lentils
¼ c. low-fat plain yogurt
1 minced small onion
4 c. de-boned, skinless and roasted chicken
2 tsps. Curry powder
1 ½ tsps. Canola oil
14 oz. fire-roasted diced tomatoes
¼ tsp. salt

Directions:
Heat oil in a large heavy saucepan over medium-high heat.
Add onion and cook, stirring, until softened but not browned, 3 to 4 minutes.
Add curry powder and cook, stirring, until combined with the onion and intensely aromatic, 20 to 30 seconds.
Stir in lentils, tomatoes, chicken and salt and cook, stirring often, until heated through.
Remove from the heat and stir in yogurt. Serve immediately.

Nutrition:
Calories: 307, Fat:6 g, Carbs:30 g, Protein:35 g, Sugars:0.1 g, Sodium:361 mg

STOVETOP BARBECUED CHICKEN BITES

Preparation Time: 10 minutes| Servings: 4

Ingredients:

1 diced medium bell pepper
1 tbsp. canola oil
1 c. tangy, spicy, and sweet barbecue sauce
Freshly ground black pepper
1 diced medium onion
1 lb. de-boned skinless chicken breasts
3 minced garlic cloves

Directions:

Wash chicken breasts and pat dry. Cut into bite-sized chunks.

Heat oil in a large sauté pan over medium heat. Add chicken, onion, garlic, and bell pepper, and cook, stirring, for 5 minutes.

Add the barbecue sauce and stir to combine. Reduce heat to medium-low and cover pan. Cook, stirring frequently, until chicken is fully cooked, about 15 minutes.

Remove from heat. Season to taste with freshly ground black pepper and serve immediately.

Nutrition:

Calories: 191, Fat:5 g, Carbs:8 g, Protein:27 g, Sugars:0 g, Sodium:480 mg

PEACH CHICKEN TREAT

Preparation Time: 30-35 minsServings: 4-5

Ingredients:

2 minced garlic cloves
¼ c. balsamic vinegar
4 sliced peaches
4 skinless, deboned chicken breasts
¼ c. chopped basil
1 tbsp. olive oil
1 chopped shallot
¼ tsp. black pepper

Directions:

Heat up the oil in a saucepan over medium-high flame.

Add the meat and season with black pepper; fry for 8 minutes on each side and set aside to rest in a plate.

In the same pan, add the shallot and garlic; stir and cook for 2 minutes.

Add the peaches; stir and cook for 4-5 more minutes.

Add the vinegar, cooked chicken, and basil; toss and simmer covered for 3-4 minutes more. Serve warm.

Nutrition:

Calories: 270, Fat:0 g, Carbs:6.6 g, Protein:1.5 g, Sugars:24 g, Sodium:87 mg

Baked Chicken Pesto

Preparation Time: 10 mins |Servings: 4

Ingredients:
- 2 thinly sliced medium tomato
- 4 tsps. Basil pesto
- 6 tbsps. Shredded reduced fat mozzarella cheese
- 2 small de-boned, skinless chicken breast halves
- 4 tsps. grated parmesan cheese

Directions:

In cold water, wash chicken and dry using a paper towel. Create 4 thin slices out of chicken breasts by slicing horizontally.

At 400 0F, preheat oven then line a baking sheet with foil.

Put into the baking sheet the slices of chicken and spread at least 1 teaspoon of pesto on each chicken slice.

For 15 minutes, bake the chicken and ensure that the center is no longer pink. After which remove the baking sheet from the oven and top the chicken with parmesan cheese, mozzarella, and tomatoes.

Put into oven once again and heat for another 5 minutes to melt the cheese

Serve and enjoy.

Nutrition:
Calories: 163, Fat:5.9 g, Carbs:3.26 g, Protein:23.9 g, Sugars:1.8 g, Sodium:655 mg

Chicken and Avocado Bake

Preparation Time: 10 minsServings: 4

Ingredients:
- 2 thinly sliced green onion stalks
- Mashed avocado
- 170 g non-fat Greek yogurt
- 1 ¼ g salt
- 4 chicken breasts
- 15 g blackened seasoning

Directions:

Start by putting your chicken breast in a plastic zip lock bag with the blackened seasoning. Close and shake, then marinate for about 2-5 minutes.

As your chicken is marinating, go ahead and put your Greek Yogurt, mashed avocado, and salt in your blender and pulse until smooth.

Place a large skillet or cast-iron pan on the stove at medium heat, oil the pan and cook the chicken until it is cooked through. You'll need about 5 minutes on each side. However, try not to dry the juices and plate it as soon as the meat is cooked.

Top with the yogurt mixture.

Nutrition:
Calories: 296, Fat:13.5 g, Carbs:6.6 g, Protein:35.37 g, Sugars:0.8 g, Sodium:173 mg

Chicken Chopstick

Preparation Time: 45 mins Servings: 4

Ingredients:
¼ c. diced chopped onion
1 pack cooked chow Mein noodles
Fresh ground pepper
2 cans cream mushroom soup
1 ¼ c. sliced celery
1 c. cashew nuts
2 c. cubed cooked chicken
½ c. water

Directions:
Preheat the oven to 375 ° F.
In a pot suitable for the oven, pour in both cans of cream of mushroom soup and water. Mix until combined.
Add the cooked cubed chicken, onion, celery, pepper, cashew nuts to the soup. Stir until combined. Add half the noodles to the mixture, stir until coated.
Top the casserole with the rest of the noodles.
Place the pot in the oven. Bake for 25 minutes.
Serve immediately.

Nutrition:
Calories: 201, Fat:17 g, Carbs:15 g, Protein:13 g, Sugars:7 g, Sodium:10 mg

Champion Chicken Pockets

Preparation Time: 5 mins Servings: 4

Ingredients:
½ c. chopped broccoli
2 halved whole wheat pita bread rounds
¼ c. bottled reduced-fat ranch salad dressing
¼ c. chopped pecans or walnuts
1 ½ c. chopped cooked chicken
¼ c. plain low-fat yogurt
¼ c. shredded carrot

Directions:
In a small bowl stir together yogurt and ranch salad dressing.
In a medium bowl combine chicken, broccoli, carrot, and, if desired, nuts. Pour yogurt mixture over chicken; toss to coat.
Spoon chicken mixture into pita halves.

Nutrition:
Calories: 384, Fat:11.4 g, Carbs:7.4 g, Protein:59.3 g, Sugars:1.3 g, Sodium:368.7 mg

Chapter 14. Seafood

Lemony Mussels

Preparation Time: 5 mins Servings: 4
Ingredients:
1 tbsp. extra virgin extra virgin olive oil
2 minced garlic cloves
2 lbs. scrubbed mussels
Juice of one lemon
Directions:
Put some water in a pot, add mussels, bring with a boil over medium heat, cook for 5 minutes, discard unopened mussels and transfer them with a bowl.
In another bowl, mix the oil with garlic and freshly squeezed lemon juice, whisk well, and add over the mussels, toss and serve.
Enjoy!
Nutrition:
Calories: 140, Fat:4 g, Carbs:8 g, Protein:8 g, Sugars: 4g, Sodium:600 mg,

Hot Tuna Steak

Preparation Time: 10 mins Servings: 6
Ingredients:
2 tbsps. Fresh lemon juice
Pepper.
Roasted orange garlic mayonnaise
¼ c. whole black peppercorns
6 sliced tuna steaks
2 tbsps. Extra-virgin olive oil
Salt
Directions:
Place the tuna in a bowl to fit. Add the oil, lemon juice, salt and pepper. Turn the tuna to coat well in the marinade. Let rest 15 to 20 minutes, turning once.
Place the peppercorns in a double thickness of plastic bags. Tap the peppercorns with a heavy saucepan or small mallet to crush them coarsely. Place on a large plate.
When ready to cook the tuna, dip the edges into the crushed peppercorns. Heat a nonstick skillet over medium heat. Sear the tuna steaks, in batches if necessary, for 4 minutes per side for medium-rare fish, adding 2 to 3 tablespoons of the marinade to the skillet if necessary, to prevent sticking.
Serve dolloped with roasted orange garlic mayonnaise
Nutrition:
Calories: 124, Fat:0.4 g, Carbs:0.6 g, Protein:28 g, Sugars:0 g, Sodium:77 mg

Marinated Fish Steaks

Preparation Time: 10 mins Servings: 4
Ingredients:
4 lime wedges
2 tbsps. Lime juice
2 minced garlic cloves
2 tsps. Olive oil
1 tbsp. snipped fresh oregano
1 lb. fresh swordfish
1 tsp. lemon-pepper seasoning

Directions:
Rinse fish steaks; pat dry with paper towels. Cut into four serving size pieces, if necessary.
In a shallow dish combine lime juice, oregano, oil, lemon-pepper seasoning, and garlic. Add fish; turn to coat with marinade.
Cover and marinate in refrigerator for 30 minutes to 1-1/2 hours, turning steaks occasionally. Drain fish, reserving marinade.
Place fish on the greased unheated rack of a broiler pan.
Broil 4 inches from the heat for 8 to 12 minutes or until fish begins to flake when tested with a fork, turning once and brushing with reserved marinade halfway through cooking. Discard any remaining marinade.
Before serving, squeeze the juice from one lime wedge over each steak.

Nutrition:
Calories: 240, Fat:6 g, Carbs:19 g, Protein:12 g, Sugars:3.27 g, Sodium:325 mg

Baked Tomato Hake

Preparation Time: 35-40 mins Servings: 4-5
Ingredients:
½ c. tomato sauce
1 tbsp. olive oil
Parsley
2 sliced tomatoes
½ c. grated cheese
4 lbs. de-boned and sliced hake fish
Salt.

Directions:
Preheat the oven to 400 0F.
Season the fish with salt.
In a skillet or saucepan; stir-fry the fish in the olive oil until half-done.
Take four foil papers to cover the fish.
Shape the foil to resemble containers; add the tomato sauce into each foil container.
Add the fish, tomato slices, and top with grated cheese.
Bake until you get a golden crust, for approximately 20-25 minutes.
Open the packs and top with parsley.

Nutrition:
Calories: 265, Fat:15 g, Carbs:18 g, Protein:22 g, Sugars:0.5 g, Sodium:94.6 mg

Cheesy Tuna Pasta

Preparation Time: 5-8 Minutes Servings: 3-4

Ingredients:
- 2 c. arugula
- ¼ c. chopped green onions
- 1 tbs. red vinegar
- 5 oz. drained canned tuna
- ¼ tsp. black pepper
- 2 oz. cooked whole-wheat pasta
- 1 tbsp. olive oil
- 1 tbsp. grated low-fat parmesan

Directions:

Cook the pasta in unsalted water until ready. Drain and set aside.

In a bowl of large size, thoroughly mix the tuna, green onions, vinegar, oil, arugula, pasta, and black pepper.

Toss well and top with the cheese.

Serve and enjoy.

Nutrition:

Calories: 566.3, Fat:42.4 g, Carbs:18.6 g, Protein:29.8 g, Sugars:0.4 g, Sodium:688.6 mg

Herb-Coated Baked Cod with Honey

Preparation Time: 5 mins Servings: 2

Ingredients:
- 6 tbsps. Herb-flavored stuffing
- 8 oz. cod fillets
- 2 tbsps. Honey

Directions:

Preheat your oven to 375 0F.

Spray a baking pan lightly with cooking spray.

Put the herb-flavored stuffing in a bag and close. Squash the stuffing until it gets crumbly.

Coat the fishes with honey and get rid of the remaining honey. Add one fillet to the bag of stuffing and shake gently to coat the fish completely.

Transfer the cod to the baking pan and repeat the process for the second fish.

Wrap the fillets with foil and bake until firm and opaque all through when you test with the tip of a knife blade, about ten minutes.

Serve hot.

Nutrition:

Calories: 185, Fat:1 g, Carbs:23 g, Protein:21 g, Sugars:2 g, Sodium:144.3 mg

Tender Salmon in Mustard Sauce

Preparation Time: 10 mins Servings: 2
Ingredients:
5 tbsps. Minced dill
2/3 c. sour cream
Pepper.
2 tbsps. Dijon mustard
1 tsp. garlic powder
5 oz. salmon fillets
2-3 tbsps. Lemon juice
Directions:
Mix sour cream, mustard, lemon juice and dill.
Season the fillets with pepper and garlic powder.
Arrange the salmon on a baking sheet skin side down and cover with the prepared mustard sauce.
Bake for 20 minutes at 390°F.
Nutrition:
Calories: 318, Fat:12 g, Carbs:8 g, Protein:40.9 g, Sugars:909.4 g, Sodium:1.4 mg

Broiled White Sea Bass

Preparation Time: 5 mins Servings: 2
Ingredients:
1 tsp. minced garlic
Ground black pepper
1 tbsp. lemon juice
8 oz. white sea bass fillets
¼ tsp. salt-free herbed seasoning blend
Directions:
Preheat the broiler and position the rack 4 inches from the heat source.
Lightly spray a baking pan with cooking spray. Place the fillets in the pan. Sprinkle the lemon juice, garlic, herbed seasoning and pepper over the fillets.
Broil until the fish is opaque throughout when tested with a tip of a knife, about 8 to 10 minutes.
Serve immediately.
Nutrition:
Calories: 114, Fat:2 g, Carbs:2 g, Protein:21 g, Sugars:0.5 g, Sodium:78 mg

STEAMED FISH BALL

Preparation Time: 10 minsServings: 2
Ingredients:
2 whisked eggs
2 tbsps. Rinsed and cooked rice
Salt.
10 oz. minced white fish fillets
Directions:
Combine the minced fish with the rice.
Add eggs, season with salt and stir well.
Form the balls. Arrange in a steamer basket.
Place the basket in a pot with 1 inch of water.
Steam, covered, for 30 minutes or until soft.
Nutrition:
Calories: 169, Fat:4.3 g, Carbs:1.1 g, Protein:5.3 g, Sugars:0 g, Sodium:173.1 mg

SPICY BAKED FISH

Preparation Time: 5 minsServings: 5
Ingredients:
1 tbsp. olive oil
1 tsp. spice salt free seasoning
1 lb. salmon fillet
Directions:
Preheat the oven to 350F.
Sprinkle the fish with olive oil and the seasoning.
Bake for 15 min uncovered.
Slice and serve.
Nutrition:
Calories: 192, Fat:11 g, Carbs:14.9 g, Protein:33.1 g, Sugars:0.3 g, Sodium:505 6 mg

LEMONY & CREAMY TILAPIA

Preparation Time: 15 minsServings: 4
Ingredients:
2 tbsps. Chopped fresh cilantro
¼ c. low-fat mayonnaise
Freshly ground black pepper
¼ c. fresh lemon juice
4 tilapia fillets
½ c. grated low-fat parmesan cheese
½ tsp. garlic powder
Directions:
In a bowl, mix together all ingredients except tilapia fillets and cilantro.
Coat the fillets with mayonnaise mixture evenly.
Place the filets onto a large foil paper. Wrap the foil paper around fillets to seal them.
Arrange the foil packet in the bottom of a large slow cooker.
Set the slow cooker on low.
Cover and cook for 3-4 hours.
Serve with the garnishing of cilantro.
Nutrition:
Calories: 133.6, Fat:2.4 g, Carbs:4.6 g, Protein:22 g, Sugars:0.9 g, Sodium:510.4 mg

SMOKED TROUT SPREAD

Preparation Time: 5 mins Servings: 2

Ingredients:
2 tsps. Fresh lemon juice
½ c. low-fat cottage cheese
1 diced celery stalk
¼ lb. skinned smoked trout fillet,
½ tsp. Worcestershire sauce
1 tsp. hot pepper sauce
¼ c. coarsely chopped red onion

Directions:
Combine the trout, cottage cheese, red onion, lemon juice, hot pepper sauce and Worcestershire sauce in a blender or food processor.
Process until smooth, stopping to scrape down the sides of the bowl as needed.
Fold in the diced celery.
Keep in an air-tight container in the refrigerator.

Nutrition:
Calories: 57, Fat:4 g, Carbs:1 g, Protein:4 g, Sugars:0 g, Sodium:660 mg

BROILED SEA BASS

Preparation Time: 10 mins Servings: 2

Ingredients:
2 minced garlic cloves
Pepper.
1 tbsp. lemon juice
2 white sea bass fillets
¼ tsp. herb seasoning blend

Directions:
Spray a broiler pan with some olive oil and place the fillets on it.
Sprinkle the lemon juice, garlic and the spices over the fillets.
Broil for about 10 min or until the fish is golden.
Serve over a bed of sautéed spinach if desired.

Nutrition:
Calories: 169, Fat:9.3 g, Carbs:0.34 g, Protein:15.3 g, Sugars:0.2 g, Sodium:323 mg

SPICY COD

Preparation Time: 29 mins Servings: 4

Ingredients:
2 tbsps. Fresh chopped parsley
2 lbs. cod fillets
2 c. low sodium salsa
1 tbsp. flavorless oil

Directions:
Preheat the oven to 350 ° F.
In a large, deep baking dish drizzle the oil along the bottom. Place the cod fillets in the dish.
Pour the salsa over the fish. Cover with foil for 20 minutes. Remove the foil last 10 minutes of cooking.
Bake in the oven for 20 – 30 minutes, until the fish is flaky.
Serve with white or brown rice. Garnish with parsley.

Nutrition:
Calories: 110, Fat:11 g, Carbs:83 g, Protein:16.5 g, Sugars:0 g, Sodium:122 mg

Lemon Salmon with Kaffir Lime

Preparation Time: 40 mins Servings: 8

Ingredients:

1 quartered and bruised lemon grass stalk
2 kaffir torn lime leaves
1 thinly sliced lemon
1 ½ c. fresh coriander leaves
1 whole side salmon fillet

Directions:

Pre-heat the oven to 350 ° F.

Cover a baking pan with foil sheets, overlapping the sides

Place the Salmon on the foil, top with the lemon, lime leaves, the lemon grass and 1 cup of the coriander leaves. Option: season with salt and pepper.

Bring the long side of the foil to the center before folding the seal. Roll the ends in order to close up the salmon.

Bake for 30 minutes.

Transfer the cooked fish to a platter. Top with fresh coriander. Serve with white or brown rice.

Nutrition:

Calories: 103, Fat:11.8 g, Carbs:43.5 g, Protein:18 g, Sugars:0.7 g, Sodium:322 mg

Heartfelt Tuna Melt

Preparation Time: 10 mins Servings: 4

Ingredients:

3 oz. grated reduced-fat cheddar cheese
1/3 c. chopped celery
Black pepper and salt
¼ c. chopped onion
2 whole-wheat English muffins
6 oz. drained white tuna
¼ c. low fat Russian

Directions:

Preheat broiler. Combine tuna, celery, onion and salad dressing.

Season with salt and pepper.

Toast English muffin halves.

Place split-side-up on baking sheet and top each with 1/4 of tuna mixture.

Broil 2-3 minutes or until heated through.

Top with cheese and return to broiler until cheese is melted, about 1 minute longer.

Nutrition:

Calories: 320, Fat:16.7 g, Carbs:17.1 g, Protein:25.7 g, Sugars:5.85 g, Sodium:832 mg

CRAB SALAD

Preparation Time: 10 mins Servings: 4
Ingredients:
2 c. crab meat
1 c. halved cherry tomatoes
1 tbsp. olive oil
Black pepper
1 chopped shallot
1/3 c. chopped cilantro
1 tbsp. lemon juice
Directions:
In a bowl, combine the crab with the tomatoes and the other ingredients, toss and serve.
Nutrition:
Calories: 54, Fat:3.9 g, Carbs:2.6 g, Protein:2.3 g, Sugars:2.3 g, Sodium:462.5 mg

MINTY COD MIX

Preparation Time: 10 mins Servings: 4
Ingredients:
4 boneless cod fillets
½ c. low-sodium chicken stock
2 tbsps. olive oil
¼ tsp. black pepper
1 tbsp. chopped mint
1 tsps. grated lemon zest
¼ c. chopped shallot
1 tbsp. lemon juice
Directions:
Heat up a pan with the oil over medium heat, add the shallots, stir and sauté for 5 minutes.
Add the cod, the lemon juice and the other ingredients, bring to a simmer and cook over medium heat for 12 minutes.
Divide everything between plates and serve.
Nutrition:
Calories: 160, Fat:8.1 g, Carbs:2 g, Protein:20.5 g, Sugars:8 g, Sodium:45 mg

SALMON AND DILL CAPERS

Preparation Time: 10 mins Servings: 4
Ingredients:
1 tbsp. drained capers
2 tbsps. olive oil
1 tbsp. chopped dill
½ c. coconut cream
¼ tsp. black pepper
4 boneless salmon fillets
1 chopped shallot
Directions:
Heat up a pan with the oil over medium-high heat, add the shallot and the capers, toss and sauté for 4 minutes.
Add the salmon and cook it for 3 minutes on each side.
Add the rest of the ingredients, cook everything for 5 minutes more, divide between plates and serve.
Nutrition:
Calories: 369, Fat:25.2 g, Carbs:2.7 g, Protein:35.5g, Sugars:0.1 g, Sodium:311.2 mg

CREAMY SEA BASS MIX

Preparation Time: 10 minsServings: 4
Ingredients:
1 tbsp. chopped parsley
2 tbsps. avocado oil
1 c. coconut cream
1 tbsp. lime juice
1 chopped yellow onion
¼ tsp. black pepper
4 boneless sea bass fillets
Directions:
Heat up a pan with the oil over medium heat, add the onion, toss and sauté for 2 minutes. Add the fish and cook it for 4 minutes on each side.
Add the rest of the ingredients, cook everything for 4 minutes more, divide between plates and serve.
Nutrition:
Calories: 283, Fat:12.3 g, Carbs:12.5 g, Protein:8 g, Sugars:6 g, Sodium:508.8 mg

TUNA AND SHALLOTS

Preparation Time: 10 minsServings: 4
Ingredients:
½ c. low-sodium chicken stock
1 tbsp. olive oil
4 boneless and skinless tuna fillets
2 chopped shallots
1 tsp. sweet paprika
2 tbsps. lime juice
¼ tsp. black pepper
Directions:
Heat up a pan with the oil over medium-high heat, add shallots and sauté for 3 minutes. Add the fish and cook it for 4 minutes on each side.
Add the rest of the ingredients, cook everything for 3 minutes more, divide between plates and serve.
Nutrition:
Calories: 4040, Fat:34.6 g, Carbs:3 g, Protein:21.4 g, Sugars:0.5 g, Sodium:1000 mg

PAPRIKA TUNA

Preparation Time: 4 minsServings: 4
Ingredients:
½ tsp. chili powder
2 tsps. sweet paprika
¼ tsp. black pepper
2 tbsps. olive oil
4 boneless tuna steaks
Directions:
Heat up a pan with the oil over medium-high heat, add the tuna steaks, season with paprika, black pepper and chili powder, cook for 5 minutes on each side, divide between plates and serve with a side salad.
Nutrition:
Calories: 455, Fat:20.6 g, Carbs:0.8 g, Protein:63.8 g, Sugars:7.4 g, Sodium: 411 mg

GINGER SEA BASS MIX

Preparation Time: 10 minsServings: 4
Ingredients:
4 boneless sea bass fillets
2 tbsps. olive oil
1 tsp. grated ginger
1 tbsp. chopped cilantro
Black pepper
1 tbsp. balsamic vinegar
Directions:
Heat up a pan with the oil over medium heat, add the fish and cook for 5 minutes on each side.
Add the rest of the ingredients, cook everything for 5 minutes more, divide everything between plates and serve.
Nutrition:
Calories: 267, Fat:11.2 g, Carbs:1.5 g, Protein:23 g, Sugars:0.78 g, Sodium:321.2 mg

PARMESAN COD MIX

Preparation Time: 10 minsServings: 4
Ingredients:
1 tbsp. lemon juice
½ c. chopped green onion
4 boneless cod fillets
3 minced garlic cloves
1 tbsp. olive oil
½ c. shredded low-fat parmesan cheese
Directions:
Heat up a pan with the oil over medium heat, add the garlic and the green onions, toss and sauté for 5 minutes.
Add the fish and cook it for 4 minutes on each side.
Add the lemon juice, sprinkle the parmesan on top, cook everything for 2 minutes more, divide between plates and serve.
Nutrition:
Calories: 275, Fat:22.1 g, Carbs:18.2 g, Protein:12 g, Sugars:0.34 g, Sodium:285.4 mg

Chapter 15. Meat Recipes

Lime Pork and Green Beans
Preparation time: 10 minutes
Cooking time: 40 minutes
Servings: 4
Ingredients:
2 pounds pork stew meat, cubed
2 tablespoons avocado oil
½ cup green beans, trimmed and halved
2 tablespoons lime juice
1 cup coconut milk
1 tablespoon rosemary, chopped
A pinch of salt and black pepper
Directions:
Heat up a pan with the oil over medium heat, add the meat and brown for 5 minutes.
Add the rest of the ingredients, toss gently, bring to a simmer and cook over medium heat for 35 minutes more.
Divide the mix between plates and serve.
Nutrition: calories 260, fat 5, fiber 8, carbs 9, protein 13

Pork with Lemongrass
Preparation time: 10 minutes
Cooking time: 30 minutes
Servings: 4
Ingredients:
4 pork chops
2 tablespoons olive oil
2 spring onions, chopped
A pinch of salt and black pepper
½ cup vegetable stock
1 stalk lemongrass, chopped
2 tablespoons coconut aminos
2 tablespoons cilantro, chopped
Directions:
Heat up a pan with the oil over medium-high heat, add the spring onions and the meat and brown for 5 minutes.
Add the rest of the ingredients, toss, and cook everything over medium heat for 25 minutes more.
Divide the mix between plates and serve.
Nutrition: calories 290, fat 4, fiber 6, carbs 8, protein 14

Pork with Olives

Preparation time: 10 minutes
Cooking time: 40 minutes
Servings: 4
Ingredients:
1 yellow onion, chopped
4 pork chops
2 tablespoons olive oil
1 tablespoon sweet paprika
2 tablespoons balsamic vinegar
¼ cup kalamata olives, pitted and chopped
1 tablespoon cilantro, chopped
A pinch of sea salt and black pepper
Directions:
Heat up a pan with the oil over medium heat, add the onion and sauté for 5 minutes.
Add the meat and brown for 5 minutes more.
Add the rest of the ingredients, toss, cook over medium heat for 30 minutes, divide between plates and serve.
Nutrition: calories 280, fat 11, fiber 6, carbs 10, protein 21

Pork Chops with Tomato Salsa

Preparation time: 10 minutes
Cooking time: 15 minutes
Servings: 4
Ingredients:
4 pork chops
1 tablespoon olive oil
4 scallions, chopped
1 teaspoon cumin, ground
½ tablespoon hot paprika
1 teaspoon garlic powder
A pinch of sea salt and black pepper
1 small red onion, chopped
2 tomatoes, cubed
2 tablespoons lime juice
1 jalapeno, chopped
¼ cup cilantro, chopped
1 tablespoon lime juice
Directions:
Heat up a pan with the oil over medium heat, add the scallions and sauté for 5 minutes.
Add the meat, cumin paprika, garlic powder, salt and pepper, toss, cook for 5 minutes on each side and divide between plates.
In a bowl, combine the tomatoes with the remaining ingredients, toss, divide next to the pork chops and serve.
Nutrition: calories 313, fat 23.7, fiber 1.7, carbs 5.9, protein 19.2

Mustard Pork Mix

Preparation time: 10 minutes
Cooking time: 35 minutes
Servings: 4
Ingredients:
2 shallots, chopped
1 pound pork stew meat, cubed
2 garlic cloves, minced
2 tablespoons olive oil
¼ cup Dijon mustard
2 tablespoons chives, chopped
1 teaspoon cumin, ground
1 teaspoon rosemary, dried
A pinch of sea salt and black pepper
Directions:
Heat up a pan with the oil over medium-high heat, add the shallots and sauté for 5 minutes.
Add the meat and brown for 5 minutes more.
Add the rest of the ingredients, toss, cook over medium heat for 25 minutes more.
Divide the mix between plates and serve.
Nutrition: calories 280, fat 14.3, fiber 6, carbs 11.8, protein 17

Pork with Chili Zucchinis and Tomatoes

Preparation time: 10 minutes
Cooking time: 35 minutes
Servings: 4
Ingredients:
2 tomatoes, cubed
2 pounds pork stew meat, cubed
4 scallions, chopped
2 tablespoons olive oil
1 zucchini, sliced
Juice of 1 lime
2 tablespoons chili powder
½ tablespoons cumin powder
A pinch of sea salt and black pepper
Directions:
Heat up a pan with the oil over medium heat, add the scallions and sauté for 5 minutes.
Add the meat and brown for 5 minutes more.
Add the tomatoes and the other ingredients, toss, cook over medium heat for 25 minutes more, divide between plates and serve.
Nutrition: calories 300, fat 5, fiber 2, carbs 12, protein 14

Pork with Thyme Sweet Potatoes

Preparation time: 10 minutes
Cooking time: 35 minutes
Servings: 4
Ingredients:
2 sweet potatoes, peeled and cut into wedges
4 pork chops
3 spring onions, chopped
1 tablespoon thyme, chopped
2 tablespoons olive oil
4 garlic cloves, minced
A pinch of sea salt and black pepper
½ cup vegetable stock
½ tablespoon chives, chopped
Directions:
In a roasting pan, combine the pork chops with the potatoes and the other ingredients, toss gently and cook at 390 degrees F for 35 minutes.
Divide everything between plates and serve.
Nutrition: calories 210, fat 12.2, fiber 5.2, carbs 12, protein 10

Pork with Pears and Ginger

Preparation time: 10 minutes
Cooking time: 35 minutes
Servings: 4
Ingredients:
2 green onions, chopped
2 tablespoons avocado oil
2 pounds pork roast, sliced
½ cup coconut aminos
1 tablespoon ginger, minced
2 pears, cored and cut into wedges
¼ cup vegetable stock
1 tablespoon chives, chopped
Directions:
Heat up a pan with the oil over medium heat, add the onions and the meat and brown for 2 minutes on each side.
Add the rest of the ingredients, toss gently and bake at 390 degrees F for 30 minutes.
Divide the mix between plates and serve.
Nutrition: calories 220, fat 13.3, fiber 2, carbs 16.5, protein 8

Parsley Pork and Artichokes

Preparation time: 10 minutes
Cooking time: 35 minutes
Servings: 4
Ingredients:
2 tablespoons balsamic vinegar
1 cup canned artichoke hearts, drained and quartered
2 tablespoons olive oil
2 pounds pork stew meat, cubed
2 tablespoons parsley, chopped
1 teaspoon cumin, ground
1 teaspoon turmeric powder
2 garlic cloves, minced
A pinch of sea salt and black pepper
Directions:
Heat up a pan with the oil over medium heat, add the meat and brown for 5 minutes.
Add the artichokes, the vinegar and the other ingredients, toss, cook over medium heat for 30 minutes, divide between plates and serve.
Nutrition: calories 260, fat 5, fiber 4, carbs 11, protein 20

Pork with Mushrooms and Cucumbers

Preparation time: 10 minutes
Cooking time: 25 minutes
Servings: 4
Ingredients:
2 tablespoons olive oil
½ teaspoon oregano, dried
4 pork chops
2 garlic cloves, minced
Juice of 1 lime
¼ cup cilantro, chopped
A pinch of sea salt and black pepper
1 cup white mushrooms, halved
2 tablespoons balsamic vinegar
Directions:
Heat up a pan with the oil over medium heat, add the pork chops and brown for 2 minutes on each side.
Add the rest of the ingredients, toss, cook over medium heat for 20 minutes, divide between plates and serve.
Nutrition: calories 220, fat 6, fiber 8, carbs 14.2, protein 20

Oregano Pork

Preparation time: 10 minutes
Cooking time: 8 hours
Servings: 4
Ingredients:
2 pounds pork roast, sliced
2 tablespoons oregano, chopped
¼ cup balsamic vinegar
1 cup tomato paste
1 tablespoon sweet paprika
1 teaspoon onion powder
2 tablespoons chili powder
2 garlic cloves, minced
A pinch of salt and black pepper
Directions:
In your slow cooker, combine the roast with the oregano, the vinegar and the other ingredients, toss, put the lid on and cook on Low for 8 hours.
Divide everything between plates and serve.
Nutrition: calories 300, fat 5, fiber 2, carbs 12, protein 24

Creamy Pork and Tomatoes

Preparation time: 10 minutes
Cooking time: 35 minutes
Servings: 4
Ingredients:
2 pounds pork stew meat, cubed
2 tablespoons avocado oil
1 cup tomatoes, cubed
1 cup coconut cream
1 tablespoon mint, chopped
1 jalapeno pepper, chopped
A pinch of sea salt and black pepper
1 tablespoon hot pepper
2 tablespoons lemon juice
Directions:
Heat up a pan with the oil over medium heat, add the meat and brown for 5 minutes.
Add the rest of the ingredients, toss, cook over medium heat for 30 minutes more, divide between plates and serve.
Nutrition: calories 230, fat 4, fiber 6, carbs 9, protein 14

Pork with Balsamic Onion Sauce

Preparation time: 10 minutes
Cooking time: 35 minutes
Servings: 4
Ingredients:
1 yellow onion, chopped
4 scallions, chopped
2 tablespoons avocado oil
1 tablespoon rosemary, chopped
1 tablespoon lemon zest, grated
2 pounds pork roast, sliced
2 tablespoons balsamic vinegar
½ cup vegetable stock
A pinch of sea salt and black pepper
Directions:
Heat up a pan with the oil over medium heat, add the onion and the scallions and sauté for 5 minutes.
Add the rest of the ingredients except the meat, stir, and simmer for 5 minutes.
Add the meat, toss gently, cook over medium heat for 25 minutes, divide between plates and serve.
Nutrition: calories 217, fat 11, fiber 1, carbs 6, protein 14

Ground Pork Pan

Preparation time: 5 minutes
Cooking time: 15 minutes
Servings: 4
Ingredients:
2 garlic cloves, minced
2 red chilies, chopped
2 tablespoons olive oil
2 pounds pork stew meat, ground
1 red bell pepper, chopped
1 green bell pepper, chopped
1 tomato, cubed
½ cup mushrooms, halved
A pinch of sea salt and black pepper
1 tablespoon basil, chopped
2 tablespoons coconut aminos
Directions:
Heat up a pan with the oil over medium heat, add the garlic, chilies, bell peppers, tomato and the mushrooms and sauté for 5 minutes.
Add the meat and the rest of the ingredients, toss, cook over medium heat for 10 minutes more, divide between plates and serve.
Nutrition: calories 200, fat 3, fiber 5, carbs 7, protein 17

Pork with Nutmeg Squash

Preparation time: 10 minutes
Cooking time: 35 minutes
Servings: 4
Ingredients:
1-pound pork stew meat, cubed
1 butternut squash, peeled and cubed
1 yellow onion, chopped
2 tablespoons olive oil
2 garlic cloves, minced
½ teaspoon garam masala
½ teaspoon nutmeg, ground
1 teaspoon chili flakes, crushed
1 tablespoon balsamic vinegar
A pinch of sea salt and black pepper
Directions:
Heat up a pan with the oil over medium-high heat, add the onion and the garlic and sauté for 5 minutes.
Add the meat and brown for another 5 minutes.
Add the rest of the ingredients, toss, cook over medium heat for 25 minutes, divide between plates and serve.
Nutrition: calories 348, fat 18.2, fiber 2.1, carbs 11.4, protein 34.3

Pork with Cabbage and Kale

Preparation time: 10 minutes
Cooking time: 35 minutes
Servings: 4
Ingredients:
1-pound pork stew meat, cut into strips
2 tablespoons olive oil
1 yellow onion, chopped
A pinch of sea salt and black pepper
cup green cabbage, shredded
½ cup baby kale
2 tablespoons oregano, dried
2 tablespoons balsamic vinegar
¼ cup vegetable stock
Directions:
Heat up a pan with the oil over medium-high heat, add the onion and the meat and brown for 5 minutes.
Add the cabbage and the other ingredients, toss gently and bake everything at 390 degrees F for 30 minutes.
Divide the whole mix between plates and serve.
Nutrition: calories 331, fat 18.7, fiber 2.1, carbs 6.5, protein 34.2

Pork Salad

Preparation time: 5 minutes
Cooking time: 10 minutes
Servings: 4
Ingredients:
1-pound pork stew meat, cut into strips
3 tablespoons olive oil
4 scallions, chopped
2 tablespoons lemon juice
2 tablespoons balsamic vinegar
2 cups mixed salad greens
1 avocado, peeled, pitted and roughly cubed
1 cucumber, sliced
2 tomatoes, cubed
A pinch of salt and black pepper
Directions:
Heat up a pan with 2 tablespoons of oil over medium heat, add the scallions, the meat and the lemon juice, toss and cook for 10 minutes.
In a salad bowl, combine the salad greens with the meat and the remaining ingredients, toss and serve.
Nutrition: calories 225, fat 6.4, fiber 4, carbs 8, protein 11

Curry Pork Mix

Preparation time: 5 minutes
Cooking time: 30 minutes
Servings: 4
Ingredients:
2 tablespoon olive oil
4 scallions, chopped
2 garlic cloves, minced
2 pounds pork stew meat, cubed
2 tablespoons red curry paste
1 teaspoon chili paste
2 tablespoons balsamic vinegar
¼ cup vegetable stock
¼ cup parsley, chopped
Directions:
Heat up a pan with the oil over medium-high heat, add the scallions and the garlic and sauté for 5 minutes.
Add the meat and brown for 5 minutes more.
Add the remaining ingredients, toss, cook over medium heat for 20 minutes, divide between plates and serve.
Nutrition: calories 220, fat 3, fiber 4, carbs 7, protein 12

ITALIAN PORK
Preparation time: 10 minutes
Cooking time: 1 hour
Servings: 6
Ingredients:
2 pounds pork roast
3 tablespoons olive oil
2 teaspoons oregano, dried
1 tablespoon Italian seasoning
1 teaspoon rosemary, dried
1 teaspoon basil, dried
3 garlic cloves, minced
¼ cup vegetable stock
A pinch of salt and black pepper
Directions:
In a baking pan, combine the pork roast with the oil, the oregano and the other ingredients, toss and bake at 390 degrees F for 1 hour.
Slice the roast, divide it and the other ingredients between plates and serve.
Nutrition: calories 580, fat 33.6, fiber 0.5, carbs 2.3, protein 64.9

Chapter 16. Smoothies and beverages

Veggie Poached Eggs
Servings: 4
Preparation Time: 10 min
Cooking Time: 15 minutes
Ingredients:
2 tablespoons olive oil, divided
1-pound zucchini, quartered and sliced thinly
1 large red bell pepper, seeded and chopped
1 medium onion, chopped
1 teaspoon fresh rosemary, chopped finely
Sat, to taste
4 large organic eggs
Freshly ground black pepper, to taste
Directions:
In a big skillet, heat 1 tablespoon of oil on medium-high heat.
Add zucchini, bell pepper and onion and sauté for approximately 5-8 minutes.
Stir in rosemary and salt. With a wooden spoon, create a large well inside the center of skillet by moving the veggie mixture on the sides.
Reduce the warmth to medium. Pour remaining oil inside well.
Carefully, crack the eggs within the well. Sprinkle the eggs with salt and black pepper.
Cook for approximately 1-2 minutes. Cover the skillet and cook approximately 1-2 minutes more.
For serving, carefully, scoop the veggie mixture in 4 serving plates.
Top with an egg and serve.
Nutrition:
Calories: 403, Fat: 13g, Carbohydrates: 22g, Fiber: 10g, Protein: 29g

Baked Veggie Omelette
Servings: 4
Preparation Time: 15 minutes
Cooking Time: 20-25 minutes
Ingredients:
6 large organic eggs
Salt and freshly ground black pepper, to taste
½ cup coconut milk
½ of onion, chopped
¼ cup red bell pepper, seeded and chopped
¼ cup fresh mushrooms, sliced
1 tablespoon chives, minced
Directions:
Preheat the oven to 350 degrees F. Lightly, grease a pie dish.
In a bowl, add eggs, salt, black pepper and coconut oil and beat till well combined.
In another bowl, mix together onion, bell pepper and mushrooms.
Transfer the egg mixture in prepared pie dish evenly.
Top with vegetable mixture evenly. Sprinkle with chives evenly.
Bake approximately 20-25 minutes.
Nutrition:
Calories: 418, Fat: 12g, Carbohydrates: 28g, Fiber: 8g, Protein: 22g

Apple Omelette

Servings: 1
Preparation Time: 10 min
Cooking Time: 9 minutes
Ingredients:
2 teaspoons coconut oil, divided
½ of enormous green apple, cored and sliced thinly
¼ teaspoon ground cinnamon
1/8 teaspoon ground nutmeg
2 large organic eggs
1/8 teaspoon organic vanilla extract
Pinch of salt
Maple syrup, if desired
Directions:
In a nonstick frying pan, heat 1 teaspoon of oil on medium-low heat.
Add apple slices and sprinkle with nutmeg and cinnamon.
Cook for approximately 4-5 minutes, turning once inside middle.
Meanwhile inside a bowl, add eggs, vanilla and salt and beat till fluffy.
Add remaining oil inside the pan and let it melt completely.
Place the egg mixture over apple slices evenly.
Cook for approximately 3-4 minutes or till desired doneness.
Carefully, turn the pan over a serving plate and immediately, fold the omelet.
Serve while using drizzling of maple syrup if you like.
Nutrition:
Calories: 390, Fat: 10g, Carbohydrates: 29g, Fiber: 4g, Protein: 27g

Smoked Salmon Scramble

Servings: 1
Preparation Time: 10 minutes
Cooking Time: 5 minutes
Ingredients:
2 organic eggs
1 organic egg yolk
1 tablespoon fresh dill, chopped finely
1/8 teaspoon red pepper flakes, crushed
1/8 teaspoon garlic powder
Salt and freshly ground black pepper, to taste
2 smoked salmon pieces, chopped
1 tablespoon organic olive oil
Directions:
In a bowl, add all ingredients except salmon and oil and beat till well combined.
Stir in chopped salmon.
In a little frying pan, heat oil on medium-low heat.
Add egg mixture and cook, stirring continuously approximately 3-5 minutes or till done completely.
Serve immediately.
Nutrition:
Calories: 437, Fat: 12g, Carbohydrates: 24g, Fiber: 7g, Protein: 30g

No-Bake Veggie Frittata

Servings: 4
Preparation Time: 10 minutes
Cooking Time: 26 minutes
Ingredients:
2 tablespoons coconut oil
1 large sweet potato, peeled and cut into thin slices
1 red bell pepper, seeded and sliced
2 zucchinis, sliced
8 organic eggs
Salt and freshly ground black pepper, to taste
2 tablespoons fresh parsley, chopped finely
Directions:
Preheat the oven to broiler.
In a substantial oven proof skillet, heat oil on medium-low heat.
Add sweet potato and cook approximately 7-8 minutes.
Add bell pepper and zucchini and cook for about 3-4 minutes.
Meanwhile in a bowl, add eggs, salt and black pepper and beat till well combined.
Pour egg mixture over veggies evenly. Immediately, decrease the heat to low.
Cook for about 10 minutes or till just done.
Transfer the skillet beneath the broiler and broil approximately 3-4 minutes or till top becomes golden brown.
Cut the frittata in desired size slices. Serve while using garnishing of parsley.
Nutrition:
Calories: 458, Fat: 16g, Carbohydrates: 35g, Fiber: 9g, Protein: 32g

Choco Loco Tea Drink

Preparation Time: 10 minutesCooking Time: 0 minutesServings: 1
Ingredients:
1 1/2 cups boiling water
1 green tea bag
1 tbsp cacao powder
1 tbsp honey
¼ tsp cinnamon
½ cup almond milk
Directions:
In a large mug, add hot water and tea bag. Let it steep for 10 minutes.
Discard tea bag. Stir in honey, cinnamon and cacao powder. Mix well.
Stir in mint almond milk.
Serve and enjoy.
Nutrition:
Calories 152, Total Fat 2g, Saturated Fat 0g, Total Carbs 35g, Net Carbs 33g, Protein 2g, Sugar: 28g, Fiber 2g, Sodium 101mg, Potassium 189mg

ICED MATCHA

Preparation Time: 10 minutesCooking Time: 0 minutesServings: 1

Ingredients:

½ cup hot water

1 teaspoon matcha tea powder

½ cup organic coconut milk (or whatever dairy/non-dairy drink you prefer)

1 teaspoon of raw organic honey

Ice cubes

Directions:

In a large mug, add hot water and dissolve matcha powder. Mix well.

Mix in rest of ingredients.

Serve and enjoy.

Nutrition:

Calories 298, Total Fat 29g, Saturated Fat 4g, Total Carbs 13g, Net Carbs 10g, Protein 3g, Sugar: 10g, Fiber 3g, Sodium 21mg, Potassium 320mg

TURMERIC-SPICED COCONUT MILK SHAKE

Preparation Time: 10 minutesCooking Time: 0 minutesServings: 1

Ingredients:

½ tsp Turmeric Powder

¼ tsp ginger powder

¼ tsp cinnamon powder

2 tbsp flaxseed, ground

1 cup water

1 cup coconut milk

Directions:

Add all ingredients in a blender.

Blend until smooth and creamy.

Serve and enjoy.

Nutrition:

Calories 266, Total Fat 17g, Saturated Fat 2g, Total Carbs 19g, Net Carbs 13g, Protein 12g, Sugar: 13g, Fiber 6g, Sodium 116mg, Potassium 526mg

POMEGRANATE-AVOCADO SMOOTHIE

Preparation Time: 10 minutesCooking Time: 0 minutesServings: 1

Ingredients:

½ cup spinach

½ cup ice

½ tsp vanilla extract

½ tbsp. honey

½ cup Pomegranate Juice

¼ cup Greek Yogurt

½ Avocado, peeled

Directions:

Add all ingredients in a blender.

Blend until smooth and creamy.

Serve and enjoy.

Nutrition:

Calories 295, Total Fat 15g, Saturated Fat 2g, Total Carbs 36g, Net Carbs 29g, Protein 7g, Sugar: 27g, Fiber 7g, Sodium 46mg, Potassium 906mg

OATS, FLAXSEEDS AND BANANA SMOOTHIE

Preparation Time: 10 minutesCooking Time: 0 minutesServings: 1
Ingredients:
½ cup of ice
1 tsp honey
2 tsp flaxseeds
¼ cup 100% whole grain rolled oats
1/2 cup Greek Yogurt, plain
½ cup almond milk
½ banana, peeled
¼ cup kale, shredded and stems discarded
Directions:
Add all ingredients in a blender.
Blend until smooth and creamy.
Serve and enjoy.
Nutrition:
Calories 305, Total Fat 10g, Saturated Fat 2g, Total Carbs 54g, Net Carbs 46g, Protein 11g, Sugar: 30g, Fiber 8g, Sodium 147mg, Potassium 703mg

BERRY RED SMOOTHIE

Preparation Time: 10 minutesCooking Time: 0 minutesServings: 1
Ingredients:
2 tbsp cocoa powder
2 dried and pitted dates, sliced
1 cup almond milk
1 frozen banana
4 medium hulled strawberries
¾ cup raw red beets
Directions:
Add all ingredients in a blender.
Blend until smooth and creamy.
Serve and enjoy.
Nutrition:
Calories 377, Total Fat 10g, Saturated Fat 2g, Total Carbs 69, Net Carbs 58g, Protein 13g, Sugar: 45g, Fiber 11g, Sodium 188mg, Potassium 1514mg

Pineapple Banana-Oat Smoothie

Preparation Time: 10 minutesCooking Time: 0 minutesServings: 1

Ingredients:

5-6 ice cubes
¼ tsp coconut extract
½ cup diced pineapple, fresh frozen
½ banana, frozen
1 container of 5.3oz nonfat Greek yogurt
¼ cup quick cooking oats
1 cup almond milk

Directions:

In a microwave safe cup, microwave on high for 2.5 minutes the 1 cup almond milk and ¼ cup oats.
Once oats are cooked, add 2 ice cubes to cool it down quick and mix.
Then pour the rest of the ingredients in a blender and puree until mixture is smooth and creamy along with the slightly cold cooked oats.

Nutrition:

Calories 255, Total Fat 4g, Saturated Fat 2g, Total Carbs 45g, Net Carbs 41g, Protein 14g, Sugar: 29g, Fiber 4g, Sodium 123mg, Potassium 751mg

Pineapple-Lettuce Smoothie

Preparation Time: 10 minutesCooking Time: 0 minutesServings: 2

Ingredients:

¼ tsp ground cinnamon
3 dates
1 banana, peeled and frozen
2 ½ cups fresh orange juice
2 ½ cups pineapple juice
½ apple
¼ cup red leaf lettuce
½ cup Romaine lettuce

Directions:

Add all ingredients in a blender.
Blend until smooth and creamy.
Serve and enjoy.

Nutrition:

Calories 352, Total Fat 1.2g, Saturated Fat 0.1g, Total Carbs 88g, Net Carbs 81g, Protein 4.5g, Sugar: 65g, Fiber 7g, Sodium 7mg, Potassium 1206mg

Spiced Carrot Smoothie

Preparation Time: 10 minutesCooking Time: 0 minutesServings: 1
Ingredients:
1 cup spinach, optional
½ tsp ground cinnamon
½ tsp vanilla extract
1 banana, frozen
1 cup carrot, peeled and halved
1 cup almond milk
3 tbsp raisins
Directions:
Add all ingredients in a blender.
Blend until smooth and creamy.
Serve and enjoy.
Nutrition:
Calories 274, Total Fat 3g, Saturated Fat 2g, Total Carbs 53g, Net Carbs 45g, Protein 11g, Sugar: 34g, Fiber 8g, Sodium 209mg, Potassium 1329mg

Mango, Cucumber and Spinach Smoothie

Preparation Time: 10 minutesCooking Time: 0 minutesServings: 1
Ingredients:
1 cup water
1 cup orange juice, fresh
3 cups baby spinach
1 cup frozen mango, cubed and deseeded
2 apples, cored and chopped roughly
1 cucumber, ends removed and chopped roughly
Directions:
Add all ingredients in a blender.
Blend until smooth and creamy.
Serve and enjoy.
Nutrition:
Calories 455, Total Fat 2g, Saturated Fat 0.4g, Total Carbs 111g, Net Carbs 96g, Protein 8g, Sugar: 84g, Fiber 15g, Sodium 90mg, Potassium 1885mg

Grape-Avocado Smoothie

Preparation Time: 10 minutesCooking Time: 0 minutesServings: 1
Ingredients:
1 tbsp lime juice, fresh
2 tbsp avocado
6oz Greek yogurt, plain
15 pcs red or green grapes
1 pear, peeled, cored and chopped
2 cups packed spinach leaves
Directions:
Add all ingredients in a blender.
Blend until smooth and creamy.
Serve and enjoy.
Nutrition:
Calories 243, Total Fat 3g, Saturated Fat 0.5g, Total Carbs 37g, Net Carbs 30g, Protein 20g, Sugar: 26g, Fiber 7g, Sodium 111mg, Potassium 949mg

Spiced Pumpkin Smoothie

Preparation Time: 10 minutesCooking Time: 0 minutesServings: 1
Ingredients:
Ice, optional
Pinch of nutmeg
½ tsp ginger
1 tsp cinnamon
1 small frozen banana
½ cup pureed pumpkin
1 tbsp chia seeds
¼ cup rolled oats
1 cup almond milk
Directions:
Overnight or for an hour, soak chia seeds and oats in almond milk. This will give your smoothie a finer consistency.
Then, place all the ingredients in your food processor and blend ingredients until you get a smooth consistency.
Nutrition:
Calories 348, Total Fat 11g, Saturated Fat 5g, Total Carbs 61g, Net Carbs 52g, Protein 15g, Sugar: 28g, Fiber 9g, Sodium 109mg, Potassium 1238mg

Almond and Pear Smoothie

Preparation Time: 10 minutesCooking Time: 0 minutesServings: 1

Ingredients:

2-3 dates, optional
¼ tsp ground cinnamon
1 tbsp unsalted almond butter
½ cup almond milk
½ pear, deseeded
1 banana, frozen

Directions:

Add all ingredients in a blender.
Blend until smooth and creamy.
Serve and enjoy.

Nutrition:

Calories 341, Total Fat 11g, Saturated Fat 0.8g, Total Carbs 62g, Net Carbs 53g, Protein 6g, Sugar: 41g, Fiber 9g, Sodium 88mg, Potassium 826mg

Berry Nutty Smoothie

Preparation Time: 10 minutesCooking Time: 0 minutesServings: 1

Ingredients:

1 cup frozen mix berries
½ cup almond milk
¼ cup raw cashews
¼ cup quick cooking oats
1 cup packed Romaine lettuce
¼ cup packed Swiss chard, packed, chopped and stems discarded
Ice cubes or cold water - optional

Directions:

Add all ingredients in a blender.
Blend until smooth and creamy.
Serve and enjoy.

Nutrition:

Calories 269, Total Fat 10g, Saturated Fat 1.4g, Total Carbs 43g, Net Carbs 18g, Protein 6g, Sugar: 25g, Fiber 7g, Sodium 114mg, Potassium 459mg

Chapter 17. Salads Recipes

Chickpeas Salad
Preparation time: 5 minutes
Cooking time: 0 minutes
Servings: 4
Ingredients:
2 cups canned chickpeas, drained and rinsed
1 tablespoon capers, chopped
2 tablespoons lime juice
2 tablespoons olive oil
4 spring onions, chopped
1 teaspoon chili powder
1 teaspoon cumin, ground
1 tablespoon parsley, chopped
A pinch of salt and black pepper
Directions:
In a bowl, combine the chickpeas with the capers and the other ingredients, toss and serve as a side salad.
Nutrition: calories 212, fat 4, fiber 4, carbs 12, protein 6

Quinoa and Beans
Preparation time: 10 minutes
Cooking time: 30 minutes
Servings: 4
Ingredients:
1 tablespoon olive oil
1 yellow onion, chopped
1 cup quinoa
½ cup canned black beans, drained and rinsed
2 cups chicken stock
2 garlic cloves, minced
Salt and black pepper to the taste
1 tablespoon cilantro, chopped
Directions:
Heat up a pan with the olive oil over medium heat, add the onion and the garlic and sauté for 5 minutes.
Add the quinoa and the other ingredients, toss, bring to a simmer and cook over medium heat for 25 minutes.
Divide everything between plates and serve.
Nutrition: calories 212, fat 1, fiber 2, carbs 2, protein 1

Cucumber and Green Onions Salad
Preparation time: 5 minutes
Cooking time: 0 minutes
Servings: 4
Ingredients:
2 tablespoons olive oil
2 cucumbers, sliced
4 spring onions, chopped
½ cup cilantro, chopped
½ cup lemon juice
Salt and black pepper to the taste
Directions:
In a salad bowl, combine the cucumbers with the spring onions and the other ingredients, toss and serve.
Nutrition: calories 163, fat 1, fiber 2, carbs 7, protein 9

Barley and Kale
Preparation time: 5 minutes
Cooking time: 0 minutes
Servings: 4
Ingredients:
2 cups barley, cooked
1 cup baby kale
2 tablespoons almonds, chopped
2 tablespoons balsamic vinegar
1 tablespoon olive oil
1 tablespoon cilantro, chopped
Directions:
 In a bowl, mix the barley with the kale, the almonds and the other ingredients, toss and serve as a side dish.
Nutrition: calories 175, fat 3, fiber 3, carbs 5, protein 6

Herbed Mango Mix
Preparation time: 5 minutes
Cooking time: 0 minutes
Servings: 4
Ingredients:
2 mangos, peeled and chopped
2 spring onions, chopped
1 avocado, peeled, pitted and cubed
1 tablespoon olive oil
1 tablespoon chives, chopped
1 tablespoon oregano, chopped
1 tablespoon basil, chopped
2 tablespoons lemon juice
Salt and black pepper to the taste
Directions:
In a salad bowl, mix the mangos with the spring onions, the avocado and the other ingredients, toss and serve as a side dish.
Nutrition: calories 200, fat 5, fiber 7, carbs 12, protein 3

Cabbage Slaw
Preparation time: 10 minutes
Cooking time: 0 minutes
Servings: 4
Ingredients:
2 cups green cabbage, shredded
1 carrot, grated
4 dates, chopped
2 tablespoons walnuts, chopped
1 tablespoon lemon juice
2 garlic cloves, minced
1 tablespoon apple cider vinegar
3 tablespoons olive oil
1 tablespoon parsley, chopped
A pinch of salt and black pepper
Directions:
In a bowl, combine the cabbage with the carrots, dates and the other ingredients, toss and serve as a side salad.
Nutrition: calories 140, fat 3, fiber 4, carbs 5, protein 14

Cucumber with Apples Salad

Preparation time: 5 minutes
Cooking time: 0 minutes
Servings: 4
Ingredients:
2 cucumbers, sliced
1 green apple, cored and cubed
3 spring onions, chopped
3 tablespoons olive oil
4 teaspoons orange juice
A pinch of salt and black pepper
1 tablespoon mint, chopped
1 tablespoon lemon juice
Directions:
In a bowl, mix the cucumbers with the apple, spring onions and the other ingredients, toss and serve as a side salad.
Nutrition: calories 110, fat 0, fiber 3, carbs 6, protein 8

Parsley Avocado Mix

Preparation time: 5 minutes
Cooking time: 0 minutes
Servings: 4
Ingredients:
1 tablespoon olive oil
2 avocados, peeled, pitted and sliced
1 tablespoon parsley, chopped
1 tablespoon lemon juice
1 tablespoon lemon zest, grated
A pinch of salt and black pepper
Directions:
In a bowl, combine the avocados with the oil, the parsley and the other ingredients, toss and serve as a side dish.
Nutrition: calories 100, fat 0.5, fiber 1, carbs 5, protein 5

ENDIVES AND BROCCOLI
Preparation time: 10 minutes
Cooking time: 20 minutes
Servings: 4
Ingredients:
2 endives, shredded
1 cup broccoli florets
2 tablespoons olive oil
1 tablespoon walnuts, chopped
1 tablespoon almonds, chopped
2 garlic cloves, minced
1 teaspoon rosemary, dried
1 teaspoon cumin, ground
1 teaspoon chili powder
Directions:
In a roasting pan, combine the endives with the broccoli and the other ingredients, toss and bake at 380 degrees F for 20 minutes.
Divide the mix between plates and serve.
Nutrition: calories 139, fat 9.8, fiber 9.3, carbs 11.9, protein 4.9

ARUGULA SALAD
Preparation time: 5 minutes
Cooking time: 0 minutes
Servings: 4
Ingredients:
2 cups baby arugula
Juice of 1 lime
½ cup cherry tomatoes, halved
1 tablespoon olive oil
1 tablespoon balsamic vinegar
A pinch of salt and black pepper
1 tablespoon chives, chopped
Directions:
In a salad bowl, mix the arugula with the lime juice, cherry tomatoes and the other ingredients, toss and serve.
Nutrition: calories 190, fat 2, fiber 6, carbs 11, protein 7

Mint Tomatoes and Onions Mix

Preparation time: 10 minutes
Cooking time: 0 minutes
Servings: 4
Ingredients:
1-pound cherry tomatoes, halved
4 spring onions, chopped
2 tablespoons avocado oil
3 tablespoons mint, chopped
A pinch of salt and black pepper
1 red chili pepper, chopped
Directions:
In a salad bowl, mix the tomatoes with the spring onions and the other ingredients, toss and serve as a side salad.
Nutrition: calories 129, fat 3, fiber 2, carbs 8, protein 6

Radish Salad

Preparation time: 10 minutes
Cooking time: 0 minutes
Servings: 4
Ingredients:
2 cups radishes, sliced
2 spring onions, chopped
A pinch of salt and black pepper
2 tablespoons balsamic vinegar
1 tablespoon chives, chopped
1 teaspoon rosemary, dried
2 tablespoons olive oil
Directions:
In a salad bowl, mix the radishes with the spring onions, salt, pepper and the other ingredients, toss and serve as a side salad.
Nutrition: calories 110, fat 4, fiber 2, carbs 7, protein 7

Green Beans and Okra

Preparation time: 10 minutes
Cooking time: 30 minutes
Servings: 4
Ingredients:
1 cup okra, sliced
1-pound green beans, trimmed and halved
A pinch of salt and black pepper
3 scallions, chopped
2 garlic cloves, minced
3 tablespoons olive oil
1 tablespoon cilantro, chopped
Directions:
Spread the green beans and the okra on a baking sheet lined with parchment paper, add the rest of the ingredients, toss and bake at 360 degrees F for 30 minutes.
Divide the mix between plates and serve as a side dish.
Nutrition: calories 120, fat 1, fiber 1, carbs 8, protein 7

Tomato and Celery Mix

Preparation time: 10 minutes
Cooking time: 0 minutes
Servings: 4
Ingredients:
1-pound cherry tomatoes, halved
3 celery stalks, chopped
2 spring onions, chopped
A pinch of sea salt and black pepper
Juice of 1 lemon
1 tablespoon chives, chopped
A pinch of cayenne pepper
Directions:
In a salad bowl, combine the cherry tomatoes with the celery and the other ingredients, toss and serve as a side dish.
Nutrition: calories 80, fat 3, fiber 1, carbs 8, protein 5

Corn and Avocado Mix

Preparation time: 10 minutes
Cooking time: 0 minutes
Servings: 4
Ingredients:
1 cup corn
1 avocado, peeled, pitted and cubed
1 tablespoon mint, chopped
1 cup baby spinach
Juice of 1 lemon
Zest of 1 lemon, grated
1 tablespoon avocado oil
A pinch of sea salt and black pepper
Directions:
In a salad bowl, mix the corn with the avocado, the spinach and the other ingredients, toss and serve as a side dish.
Nutrition: calories 90, fat 2, fiber 1, carbs 7, protein 5

Chicken Salad with Cashew Cream

A delicious chicken salad with the creaminess of homemade cashew cream. Celery provides a crunchiness to this creamy chicken salad.
Servings: 4
Preparation Time: 20 minutes
Ingredients:
For Dressing:
1 cup raw cashews
½ cup water
1 (1-inch) pieces fresh turmeric, grated finely
2 tablespoons fresh parsley, chopped
¾ teaspoon Dijon mustard
1 tablespoon extra-virgin olive oil
2 teaspoons fresh lemon juice
2 teaspoons coconut aminos
1 teaspoon apple cider vinegar
Salt and freshly ground black pepper, to taste
For salad:
3 cups cooked chicken, chopped
1 shallot, chopped finely
2 celery ribs, chopped finely
Directions:
For cashew cream in a very blender, add cashews and water and pulse till a whipped cream like consistency forms.
For dressing in a bowl, add cashew cream and remaining dressing ingredients and mix till well combined.
In another large bowl, mix together salad ingredients.
Pour dressing over salad and toss to coat well.
Serve immediately.
Nutrition:
Calories: 464, Fat: 15g, Carbohydrates: 28g, Fiber: 10g, Protein: 37g

Chicken, Bok Choy & Jicama Salad

A chicken and veggie salad using a wonderful dressing. This yummy salad will be a fantastic addition within your salad menu list.

Servings: 4

Preparation Time: 20 or so minutes

Ingredients:

For Dressing:

1 tablespoon fresh ginger, chopped
2 tablespoons coconut cream
2 tablespoons fresh lime juice
1 tablespoon sesame oil
1 tablespoon coconut aminos
1 tablespoon fish sauce
1 teaspoon stevia powder

For Salad:

2 cups grilled chicken, chopped
6 baby Bok choy, grilled and chopped
2 scallions, chopped
½ cup jicama, chopped
¼ cup fresh cilantro, chopped
1 tablespoon sesame seeds

Directions:

For dressing in the blender, add all dressing ingredients and mix till well combined.

In another large bowl, mix together salad ingredients.

Pour dressing over salad and toss to coat well.

Serve immediately.

Nutrition:

Calories: 154, Fat: 7.5g, Carbohydrates: 3.5g, Fiber 10, Protein: 17g

Chicken & Cabbage Salad

One of the best ideas for a healthy chicken salad. This salad comes complete with a little hint of summer flavors.

Servings: 4
Preparation Time: 25 minutes
Cooking Time: 12 minutes

Ingredients:
For Chicken Marinade:
¼ cup scallion, chopped
2 tablespoons fresh ginger, minced
¼ cup coconut aminos
¼ cup olive oil
1 tablespoon honey
Salt and freshly ground black pepper, to taste
2 skinless, boneless chicken breasts

For Salad:
¼ cup balsamic vinegar
2 cups red cabbage, shredded
1 cup green cabbage, shredded
2 cups carrots, peeled and shredded
4 cups fresh kale, trimmed and chopped
3 scallions, chopped

Directions:
For chicken in a very bowl, mix together all ingredients except chicken.
In another bowl, coat chicken with 3 tablespoons of marinade.
Refrigerate to marinate approximately 30-60 minutes.
For dressing in a very bowl, mix together remaining marinade and vinegar.
Preheat the grill to medium-high heat. Grease the grill grate.
Remove chicken from refrigerator and discard any excess marinade.
Grill for about 5-6 minutes per side.
Remove from grill whilst aside to cool down the slightly.
Cut the chicken breasts in thin slices.
In a large serving bowl, mix together salad ingredients.
Add dressing and toss to coat well.
Top with chicken slices and serve.

Nutrition:
Calories: 401, Fat: 6g, Carbohydrates: 29g, Fiber: 14g, Protein: 36g

Chicken & Broccoli Salad

One of a healthy chicken salad recipe that the full family will love to consume. This salad is perfect to get a lunch.

Servings: 2
Preparation Time: 25 minutes
Cooking Time: 12 minutes
Ingredients:
For Chicken:
1 tablespoon coconut oil
½ medium onion, chopped
9-ounce boneless chicken thigh, chopped finely
1 large garlic herb, minced
1 teaspoon fresh lime zest, grated finely
1 teaspoon ground turmeric
1 teaspoon fresh lime juice
Salt and freshly ground black pepper, to taste
For Salad:
6 broccoli stalks
3 large kale leaves, trimmed and chopped
½ of avocado, peeled, pitted and chopped
2 tablespoons fresh parsley leaves, chopped
2 tablespoons fresh cilantro, chopped
2 tablespoons pumpkin seeds, toasted
For Dressing:
1 small garlic clove, grated finely
½ teaspoon Dijon mustard
3 tablespoons extra-virgin olive oil
3 tablespoons fresh lime juice
1 teaspoon raw honey
Salt and freshly ground black pepper, to taste
Directions:
In a small skillet, melt coconut oil on medium-high heat.
Add onion and sauté for approximately 4-5 minutes.
Add chicken and garlic and stir fry for about 2-3 minutes.
Add remaining ingredients and cook, stirring occasionally approximately 3-4 minutes.
Meanwhile in the pan of boiling water, add broccoli and cook for around 2 minutes.
Drain well and rinse under cold water and after that cut each stalk in 3-4 pieces.
In a bowl, add all dressing ingredients and mix till well combined.
Add kale and along with your hands rub till coated with dressing generously.
Add chicken, broccoli, avocado, herbs and pumpkin seeds and toss to coat well.
Serve immediately.
Nutrition:
Calories: 476, Fat: 17g, Carbohydrates: 31g, Fiber: 13g, Protein: 40g

BEEF & BROCCOLI SALAD

A delicious and filling dinnertime salad. Surely this filling salad would be enjoyed by the whole family.

Servings: 4
Preparation Time: 15 minutes
Cooking Time: 7 minutes

Ingredients:

For Dressing:
- 2 tablespoons shallots, minced
- 1 tablespoon fresh ginger, minced
- ½ cup extra-virgin essential olive oil
- 2 tablespoons fresh lime juice
- 1 tablespoon balsamic vinegar
- Salt and freshly ground black pepper, to taste

For Salad:
- 3 cups broccoli florets
- 1-pound beef sirloin steak, trimmed and cut into thin strips
- 1 red bell pepper, seeded and sliced thinly
- 1 red onion, sliced thinly
- 8 cups fresh baby salad greens

Directions:

In a bowl, add all dressing ingredients and beat till well combined.
Ina skillet, add 2 tablespoons of dressing as well as heat on medium-high heat.
Add broccoli and cook for about 3 minutes.
Add beef and stir fry approximately 3-4 minutes.
Remove from heat whilst aside to cool slightly.
In a big serving bowl, mix together beef mixture and remaining salad ingredients.
Add dressing and toss to coat well.

Nutrition:
Calories: 453, Fat: 11g, Carbohydrates: 27g, Fiber: 13g, Protein: 36g

Smoked Salmon & Veggie Salad

A smoked salmon and veggie salad with a light dressing. This light dressing adds and delish flavors in salad.

Servings: 2
Preparation Time: 20 minutes
Ingredients:
4 radishes, trimmed and sliced thinly
2 tomatoes, chopped
½ of cucumber, peeled and chopped
1 carrot, peeled and sliced diagonally
1 small head romaine lettuce
5-ounce smoked salmon, sliced thinly
For Dressing:
1 teaspoon fresh ginger, minced
1 tablespoon fresh lemon juice
1 tbsp. olive oil
Directions:
In a bowl, mix together radishes, tomatoes, cucumber and carrot.
In another bowl, add all dressing ingredients and beat till well combined.
Divide lettuce in serving plates and top with carrot mixture, then salmon evenly.
Pour dressing over salad and serve immediately.
Nutrition:
Calories: 447, Fat: 7g, Carbohydrates: 32g, Fiber: 16g, Protein: 31g

Salmon, Orange & Beet Salad

An amazingly delicious salad with a healthy dressing. The citrus dressing gives this salmon salad a delicious taste and texture.

Servings: 1-2
Preparation Time: 15 minutes
Ingredients:
For Salad:
6-ounce cooked salmon, chopped
1 large orange, peeled, seeded and chopped roughly
½ cup cooked beets, peeled and chopped
¼ of avocado, peeled, pitted and chopped
1 small red onion, chopped
3 cups lettuce, torn
10 pistachios, chopped
For Dressing:
½ teaspoon fresh orange zest, grated finely
2 tablespoons fresh orange juice
1 tablespoon extra-virgin olive oil
2 teaspoons balsamic vinegar
½ teaspoon Dijon mustard
¼-½ teaspoon red chili powder
Salt and freshly ground black pepper, to taste
Directions:
In a big bowl, mix together all salad ingredients.
In another bowl, add all dressing ingredients and mix till well combined.
Place dressing over quinoa mixture and mix till well combined.
Serve immediately.
Nutrition:
Calories: 453, Fat: 10g, Carbohydrates: 26g, Fiber: 15g, Protein: 30g

SALMON, SPINACH & KALE SALAD

One of the great salads with super-food ingredients. This salad comes while using healthy nutrients of salmon, spinach and kale.

Servings: 1
Preparation Time: 10 minutes
Ingredients:
For Salad:
¼ cup fresh orange juice
1 (4-ounce) salmon fillet
1 teaspoon raw honey
1½ cups fresh baby spinach
1 teaspoon coconut oil
1½ cups fresh baby kale
½ of avocado, peeled, pitted and sliced
1 orange, peeled, seeded and sectioned
3 tablespoons pomegranate seeds
For Dressing:
½ tablespoon coconut oil
1 teaspoon raw honey
2½ tablespoons fresh orange juice
Salt, to taste
Directions:
In a bowl, mix together ¼ cup of orange juice and salmon.
Refrigerate, covered for approximately a couple of hours.
Preheat the oven to 400 degrees F. Grease a tiny baking dish.
Coat each side of salmon fillet with honey evenly.
In a smaller frying pan, melt coconut oil on medium heat.
Add salmon fillet and cook for around 1-2 minutes per side.
Transfer the salmon fillet into a prepared baking dish and bake for approximately 8-10 minutes.
Meanwhile in a substantial bowl, mix together all salad ingredients.
For dressing inside a microwave safe bowl, add coconut oil and honey and microwave for approximately 20 seconds or till melted.
Add orange juice and salt and beat well.
Pour dressing over salad and toss to coat well.
Top with salmon fillet and serve.
Nutrition:
Calories: 497, Fat: 11g, Carbohydrates: 24g, Fiber: 12g, Protein: 34g

Salmon & Tomato Salad

A delicious salad which prepares in a short time without fuss. Parsley and lime juice add refreshingly tasty touch in salad.

Servings: 2
Preparation Time: 10 minutes
Ingredients:
1 (14-ounce) can salmon, flaked
1 large tomato, chopped
1 bunch fresh parsley. Chopped
1 tablespoon fresh lime juice
Freshly ground black pepper, to taste
Directions:
In a substantial bowl, add all ingredients and toss to coat well.
Refrigerate to chill before serving.
Nutrition:
Calories: 417, Fat: 5g, Carbohydrates: 24g, Fiber: 12g, Protein: 30g

SALMON & BEANS SALAD

A wonderfully flavored salad. The flavor of the salmon constitutes a wonderful combination with three beans mixture.

Servings: 4
Preparation Time: 15 minutes
Cooking Time: 7 minutes

Ingredients:
For Salmon:
4 (6-ounce) salmon fillets
Ground cumin, to taste
Salt and freshly ground black pepper, to taste
2 tablespoons olive oil

For Salad:
1 (15-ounce) can pinto beans, rinsed and drained
1 (15-ounce) can kidney beans, rinsed and drained
1 (15-ounce) can navy beans, rinsed and drained
1 medium bunch scallion, chopped
1 small bunch fresh parsley, chopped
1/3 cup extra-virgin essential olive oil
¼ cup freshly squeezed lemon juice
Salt and freshly ground black pepper, to taste

Directions:
Sprinkle the salmon fillets with cumin, salt and black pepper evenly.
In a sizable nonstick skillet, heat oil on medium heat.
Ass salmon, skin-side down and cook for about 3-4 minutes.
Carefully flip the side and cook for about 3 minutes.
Meanwhile in the bowl, mix together all salad ingredients.
Top with salmon fillets and serve.

Nutrition:
Calories: 429, Fat: 16g, Carbohydrates: 24g, Fiber: 2g, Protein: 40g

CONCLUSION

I would like to thank you again for purchasing the book and taking the time for going through the book as well.

I do hope this book was insightful and you found the information useful!

Keep in mind that you are not only limited to the recipes provided in this book. Continue to explore and experiment with healthy eating. The possibilities are endless.

Stay healthy and stay safe!